W9-ATO-844

How to Use This Book

Look for these special features in this book:

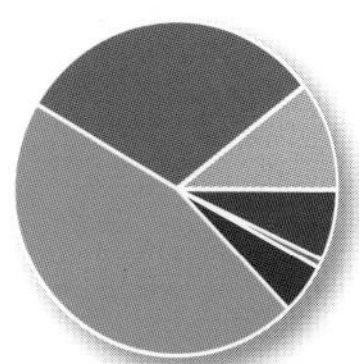

SIDEBARS, **CHARTS**, **GRAPHS**, and original **MAPS** expand your understanding of what's being discussed—and also make useful sources for classroom reports.

FAQs answer common **F**requently **A**sked **Q**uestions about people, places, and things.

WOW FACTORS offer "Who knew?" facts to keep you thinking.

TRAVEL GUIDE gives you tips on exploring the state—either in person or right from your chair!

PROJECT ROOM provides fun ideas for school assignments and incredible research projects. Plus, there's a guide to primary sources—what they are and how to cite them.

Please note: All statistics are as up-to-date as possible at the time of publication.

Consultants: William Loren Katz; Joseph T. Kelley, Chair, Department of Earth Sciences, University of Maine; Christi A. Mitchell, Staff Historian, Maine Historic Preservation Commission

Book production by The Design Lab

Library of Congress Cataloging-in-Publication Data
Heinrichs, Ann.
Maine / by Ann Heinrichs.
p. cm.—(America the beautiful. Third series)
Includes bibliographical references and index.
ISBN-13: 978-0-531-18575-9
ISBN-10: 0-531-18575-3
1. Maine—Juvenile literature. I. Title. II. Series.
F19.3.H445 2008
974.1—dc22 2007000302

1 2 3 4 5 6 7 8 9 10 R 17 16 15 14 13 12 11 10 09 08

Maine

BY ANN HEINRICHS

Third Series

Children's Press®
An Imprint of Scholastic Inc.
New York ★ Toronto ★ London ★ Auckland ★ Sydney
Mexico City ★ New Delhi ★ Hong Kong
Danbury, Connecticut

CONTENTS

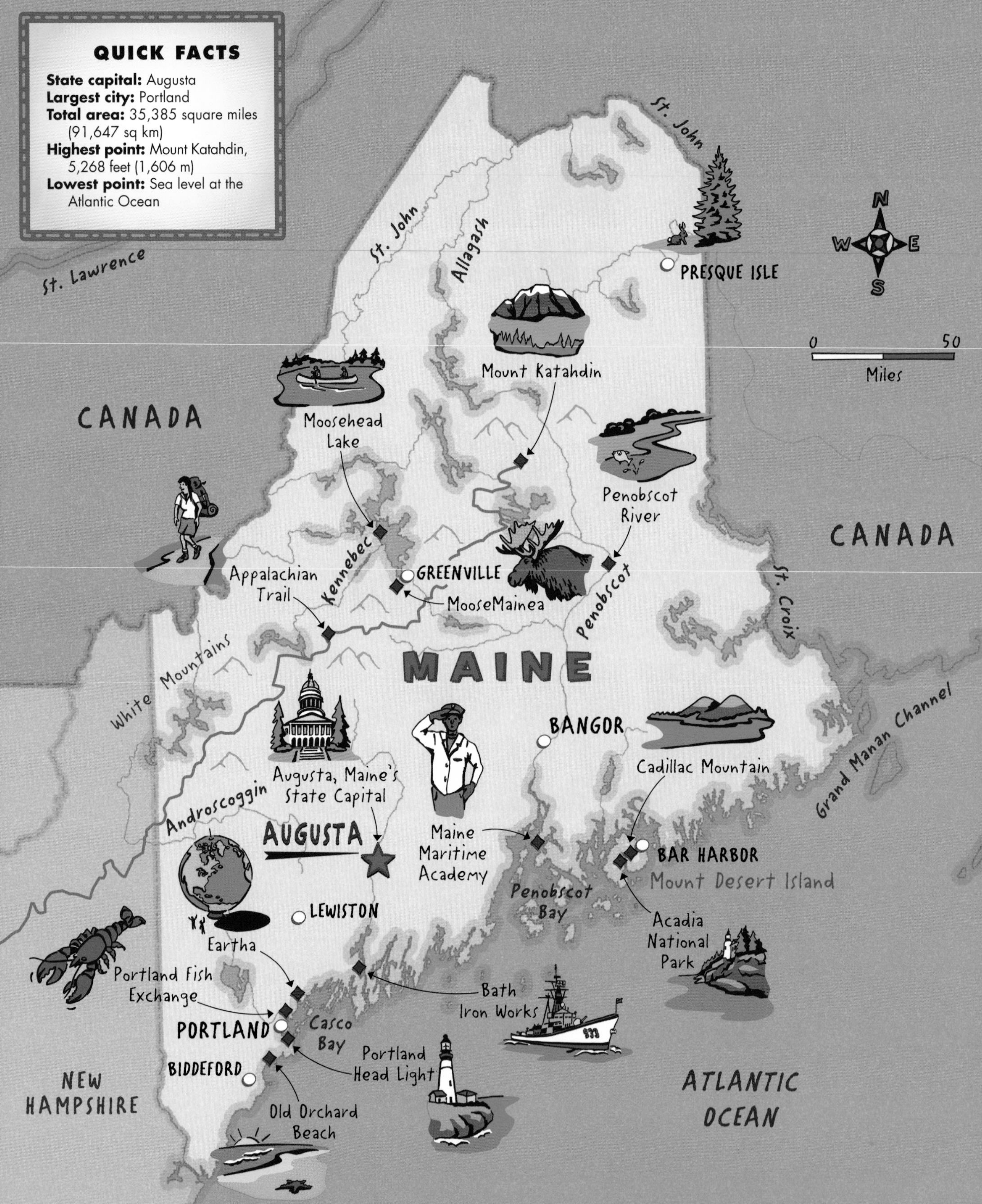
QUICK FACTS
State capital: Augusta
Largest city: Portland
Total area: 35,385 square miles (91,647 sq km)
Highest point: Mount Katahdin, 5,268 feet (1,606 m)
Lowest point: Sea level at the Atlantic Ocean
St. John
St. John
Allagash
St. Lawrence
PRESQUE ISLE
N
W
E
S
0
50
Miles
Mount Katahdin
CANADA
Moosehead Lake
Penobscot River
CANADA
Kennebec
GREENVILLE
Appalachian Trail
MooseMainea
Penobscot
St. Croix
White Mountains
MAINE
BANGOR
Grand Manan Channel
Cadillac Mountain
Augusta, Maine's State Capital
Androscoggin
AUGUSTA
Maine Maritime Academy
BAR HARBOR
Mount Desert Island
Penobscot Bay
LEWISTON
Acadia National Park
Eartha
Portland Fish Exchange
Bath Iron Works
PORTLAND
Casco Bay
Portland Head Light
BIDDEFORD
NEW HAMPSHIRE
ATLANTIC OCEAN
Old Orchard Beach

Welcome to Maine!

CANAD

HOW DID MAINE GET ITS NAME?

MAINE

The origin of Maine's name is a bit of a mystery. In fact, historians have been debating the question for more than 200 years!

Several theories have popped up over the years. One theory is that Maine was named to honor England's queen Henrietta Maria. She was said to own a French province called Maine. But this was later proved false. Other theories have come and gone. Today, many historians prefer a simple explanation. They say that sailors on the high seas called the land Maine—meaning the mainland, separate from its offshore islands. It's the perfect name for this state by the sea.

READ ABOUT

Seals sunning themselves on the rocks off Mount Desert Island

LAND

★

FOR A PLACE OF INCREDIBLE NATURAL BEAUTY, LOOK NO FARTHER THAN MAINE! This state of dramatic contrasts covers 35,385 square miles (91,647 square kilometers). Along the Atlantic Ocean, at sea level, is Maine's lowest point. There, seals rest on the shore and seabirds call overhead. On the beaches, crabs skitter among the seashells. Away from the coast, you'll find a forested wilderness with hundreds of lakes and rippling streams. Deer, bears, and moose live in these shadowy woods. Rising above them all is Mount Katahdin. At 5,268 feet (1,606 meters), it's Maine's highest point.

THE TIP OF THE NATION

Maine is located at the northeastern tip of the country. On a U.S. map, it's in the upper right-hand corner. Maine's long eastern coast faces the Atlantic Ocean. The little **peninsula** of West Quoddy Head is the easternmost point of the United States. It's part of Lubec, the country's easternmost town.

How long is Maine's coastline? That's a good question! Follow the broad outlines of the coast, and you cover only 228 miles (367 km). But if you measure along the thousands of bays and inlets, the coastline is almost 3,500 miles (5,600 km) long. Add in all the offshore islands, and you get a coastline of more than 5,300 miles (8,500 km)!

New Hampshire, to the southwest, is the only U.S. state that borders Maine. Cross Maine's northern border, and you're in Canada. To the northwest is the province of Quebec, and to the northeast is New Brunswick.

WORD TO KNOW

peninsula *a body of land surrounded by water on three sides but connected to a larger piece of land*

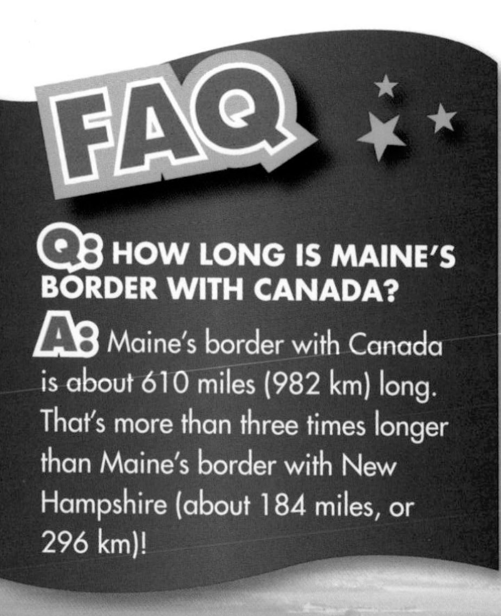

Q: HOW LONG IS MAINE'S BORDER WITH CANADA?

A: Maine's border with Canada is about 610 miles (982 km) long. That's more than three times longer than Maine's border with New Hampshire (about 184 miles, or 296 km)!

In this view from Cadillac Mountain, a cruise ship makes its way through Frenchman Bay and the Porcupine Islands and past Bar Harbor.

Maine Geo-Facts

Along with the state's geographical highlights, this chart ranks Maine's land, water, and total area compared to all other states.

Total area; rank	35,385 square miles (91,647 sq km); 39th
Land; rank	30,862 square miles (79,932 sq km); 39th
Water; rank	4,523 square miles (11,715 sq km); 12th
Inland water; rank	2,264 square miles (5,864 sq km); 9th
Coastal water; rank	.613 square miles (1,588 sq km); 9th
Territorial water; rank	1,647 square miles (4,266 sq km); 6th
Geographic center	Piscataquis County, 18 miles (29 km) north of Dover
Latitude	43° 4′ N to 47° 28′ N
Longitude	66° 57′ W to 71° 7′ W
Highest point	Mount Katahdin, 5,268 feet (1,606 m)
Lowest point	Sea level at the Atlantic Ocean
Lowest river	Kennebec, 150 miles (241 km)
Largest city	Portland
Longest River	St. John River

Source: U.S. Census Bureau

Maine is almost as big as all the other New England states put together. Rhode Island, the smallest state, would fit inside Maine almost 23 times!

Maine is in a region called New England. This was one of the first regions in North America where people from England settled. The other New England states are New Hampshire, Vermont, Massachusetts, Connecticut, and Rhode Island.

LAND REGIONS

Massive **glaciers** once covered all of Maine. As the glaciers moved along, they carried huge boulders that scraped an uneven surface onto the land. Lakes formed in gouged-out spots, and high places were smoothed off, leaving rounded hills. The weight of the glaciers pushed down the crust of the earth so much that ocean waters crept inland. Sandy areas called deltas formed in places that were once at the ocean's edge.

WORD TO KNOW

glaciers *slow-moving masses of ice*

Maine Topography

Use the color-coded elevation chart to see on the map Maine's high points (dark red to orange) and low points (green). Elevation is measured as the distance above or below sea level.

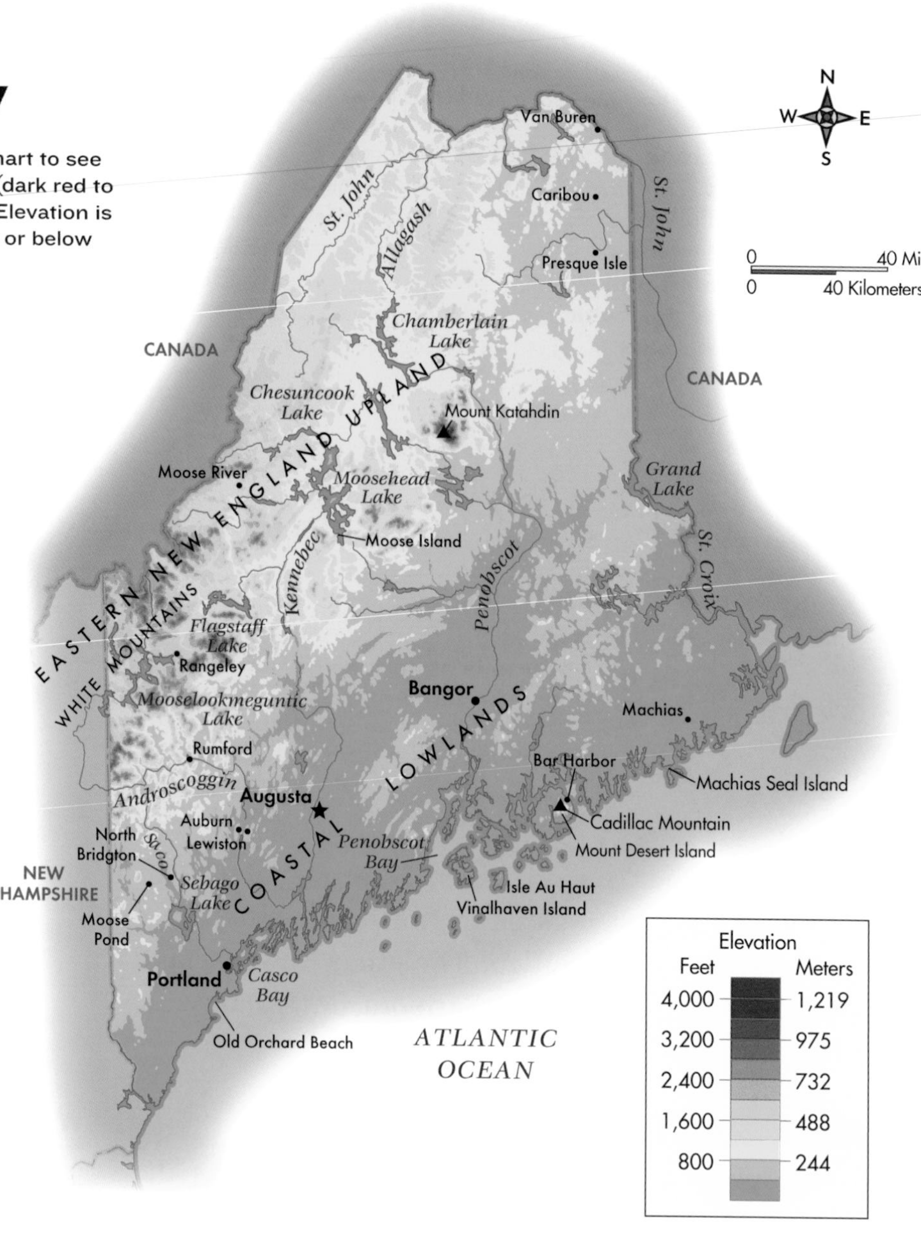

As the glaciers melted, they filled many old river valleys with debris, and new rivers appeared on the landscape. Maine's largest rivers, the Kennebec and the Penobscot, are among the youngest rivers in America. The land rebounded after the weight of the glaciers was removed and the sea level fell. Once the land attained its normal elevation, melting glaciers in Canada caused the sea level to rise hundreds of feet to approximately the present shoreline. Measurements taken at the Maine coast show a rise in sea level of more than 6 inches (15 centimeters) in the last century.

The Coastal Lowlands

Today, Maine has three major land regions. The Coastal Lowlands region runs along the coast in the southeastern part of the state. Long, sandy beaches cover the southern part of this region. Old Orchard Beach is just south of Portland, Maine's largest city. It's one of the longest, smoothest beaches on the Atlantic coast. To the north, the rocky beaches are broken by peninsulas, bays, and high cliffs.

More than 1,000 islands lie offshore. The largest is Mount Desert Island. Much of its mountainous, forested landscape is protected as Acadia National Park. The island's town of Bar Harbor is a popular summer resort. Machias Seal Island, off the northwest coast, is disputed territory. Both the United States and Canada claim it.

SEE IT HERE!

ACADIA NATIONAL PARK

Acadia National Park is the only national park in New England. It covers several islands off the coast of Maine and a long nearby peninsula (Schoodic Peninsula). Most of the park is on Mount Desert Island. There you can trek along more than 120 miles (190 km) of hiking trails. Along the way, you might see bats and peregrine falcons. Many visitors like to climb the park's rocky peaks, such as Cadillac Mountain. It's the highest point on the Atlantic coast. Stand atop the peak in the early morning, and you'll be the first person in the country to see the rising sun!

A crowd enjoys a summer day at Old Orchard Beach.

Hikers pause near the summit of Mount Katahdin, Maine's highest peak.

The White Mountain Region

Northwestern Maine is the White Mountain region. These mountains continue west into New Hampshire and Vermont. In Maine, this mountain range is called the Longfellow Mountains, after Maine poet Henry Wadsworth Longfellow. Some of these mountains are composed of granite, a hard stone used as a building material, but most are formed from **metamorphic** rocks that were once ocean mud.

Dense forests cover the rugged terrain in this part of Maine. Hundreds of lakes are scattered throughout the region. Some of the highest mountains in the state rise here, too. One is Mount Katahdin, Maine's highest peak. The top of Mount Katahdin is the end of the Appalachian Trail. This long hiking trail begins in Georgia.

WORD TO KNOW

metamorphic *describing rocks that have been changed by extreme pressure, wind, and water*

The Eastern New England Upland

Between the Coastal Lowlands and the White Mountains is the Eastern New England Upland. This is the largest geographical region in the state. It's not quite as rugged as the western mountain region, and its rolling landscape holds many rivers and lakes. Maine's best farmland is in this region, too. Aroostook County, in the far north, is best known for growing potatoes.

RIVERS AND LAKES

More than 2,500 lakes and ponds are scattered across the state. The largest is Moosehead Lake, in west-central Maine. Other large lakes are Sebago, Chesuncook, Flagstaff, Mooselookmeguntic, and Grand lakes.

More than 5,000 sparkling rivers and streams run through Maine. In the far north, the St. John and St. Croix rivers form parts of Maine's border with Canada. The Androscoggin and Saco rivers rise in New Hampshire. The Kennebec River flows out of Moosehead Lake, while the Penobscot River's waters begin in several northern lakes.

Many of Maine's industrial cities grew up along its rivers. Augusta, the state capital, lies along the Kennebec River. The cities of Lewiston and Auburn are on the Androscoggin River, and Bangor is on the Penobscot River. Indian Island lies in the Penobscot River north of Bangor. It's home to the Penobscot nation, one of Maine's Native American groups.

Would you believe Maine has a state dirt? The Chesuncook soil series is the official state soil. It's a rich material left behind by ancient glaciers.

The Bates College crew team on the Androscoggin River one autumn day

Weather Report

This chart shows record temperatures (high and low) for the state, as well as average temperatures (July and January) and average annual precipitation for Caribou and Portland.

Record high temperature . . . . 105°F (41°C) at North Bridgton on July 10, 1911
Record low temperature . . . . –48°F (–44°C) at Van Buren on January 19, 1925
Average July temperature, Caribou . . . . 66°F (19°C)
Average January temperature, Caribou. . . . . 10°F (–12°C)
Average annual precipitation, Caribou . . . . 37.4 inches (95 cm)
Average July temperature, Portland . . . . 69°F (21°C)
Average January temperature, Portland . . . . 22°F (–6°C)
Average annual precipitation, Portland . . . 45.8 inches (116 cm)

Source: National Climatic Data Center, NESDIS, NOAA, U.S. Department of Commerce

CLIMATE

Maine is generally cooler than most other states. Winters are long and cold, though the pleasant and sometimes hot summers give Maine one of its nicknames: Vacationland.

As a whole, the state gets an average of 41 inches (104 cm) of **precipitation** every year. About 25 percent of that comes in the form of snow. Maine's inland regions have colder winters than the coast, and they get more snow. Snowmobilers, snowboarders, and skiers make the most of their snowy winters. But people along the coast watch out for nor'easters (short for "northeasters"). These winter storms blow in from the northeast, bringing fierce winds, heavy snow, and sometimes floods.

Spring is a wet, soggy season. The snows melt, and the ground thaws out and turns to mud. Summers are mild, with an average July temperature of only 67

WORD TO KNOW

precipitation *all water that falls to the earth, including rain, sleet, hail, snow, dew, fog, or mist*

The Portland Head Light shrouded in fog

degrees Fahrenheit (19 degrees Celsius). Temperatures begin to drop in September. By mid-October, the brilliantly colored autumn leaves are at their peak.

Fog often drifts in from the ocean, veiling the coast in a dense haze. Many a ship has crashed on the rocky shore because sailors could not see it through the fog. Over the years, dozens of lighthouses were built on rocky peninsulas along the coast. Lighthouses use not only lights but also loud **foghorns** and clanging bells as warning signals. Mainers have a sort of affection for their lighthouses. They're a part of the state's seafaring history and culture and have saved thousands of lives.

WORD TO KNOW

foghorns *horns that blast a loud, honking sound as a signal to boaters*

Forestland near Southbranch Pond

PLANT LIFE

Forests cover almost 90 percent of Maine's land area. No other state has such a high percentage of forestland. Thanks to these trees, Maine has long had a thriving wood-products industry. Most of the wood is made into paper.

WORD TO KNOW

resource *a supply of natural material that helps people live or brings them wealth*

One of Maine's nicknames is the Pine Tree State, and the state tree is the white pine. In the 1700s, white pines were Maine's most valuable **resource**. Their tall, straight trunks were made into masts for sailing ships. White pines still grow in Maine, but the great white pine forests are not as abundant.

Spruce, fir, and hemlock trees are common in Maine's forests. Maple, beech, birch, and oak trees grow there, too. People use the sap from maple trees to make delicious maple syrup.

Lady's slipper

When spring arrives, colorful wildflowers are a welcome sight. Some of Maine's wildflowers are lady's slipper, jack-in-the-pulpit, black-eyed Susan, and lily of the valley. Common shrubs include speckled alder, witch hazel, yew, and hawthorn. Blueberries are an important Maine crop and cover large fields on the

Maine National Park Areas

This map shows some of Maine's national parks, monuments, preserves, and other areas protected by the National Park Service.

sand barrens of coastal Washington County. These barrens are deltas formed at the edge of glaciers. Throughout the state, spring is the time for picking fiddleheads along the riverbanks. These coiled leaves of the ostrich fern are a delicious taste treat.

MINI-BIO

HENRY DAVID THOREAU: INTO THE WILDERNESS

For most of his life, Henry David Thoreau (1817–1862) lived in Massachusetts. There, the author and philosopher wrote his best-known works near Walden Pond, in Concord. Thoreau believed in living a simple life surrounded by nature. That feeling drew him to Maine three times, saying he must travel "far in the recesses of the wilderness." He recorded his thoughts and experiences of Maine's mountains, waterways, and animals in his book *The Maine Woods*.

Want to know more? See www.destinationmaine.com/thoreau/history.htm

ANIMAL LIFE

Trek through the northern woods, and you may hear a deep, moaning call. It's a moose! Maine is home to a large moose population. And look at some of Maine's place-names—Moosehead Lake, Moose River, Moose Pond, Moose Island, and many others. People even go on moose-watching trips to get a glimpse of these huge animals.

Maine's forests are home to many other wild creatures. It's estimated that more than 22,000 black bears live there. White-tailed deer are another abundant animal. Smaller animals include bobcats, foxes, weasels, squirrels, chipmunks, and porcupines.

FAQ

Q: WHAT ARE SOME MOOSE FACTS?

A: The moose is the largest member of the deer family.

- Moose have no front teeth on their upper jaw.
- The flap of skin hanging below a moose's throat is called a bell.
- Only the males grow antlers. They shed their antlers in the winter and grow bigger ones in the spring.
- Moose usually live 7 to 8 years, but can live up to 25 years.

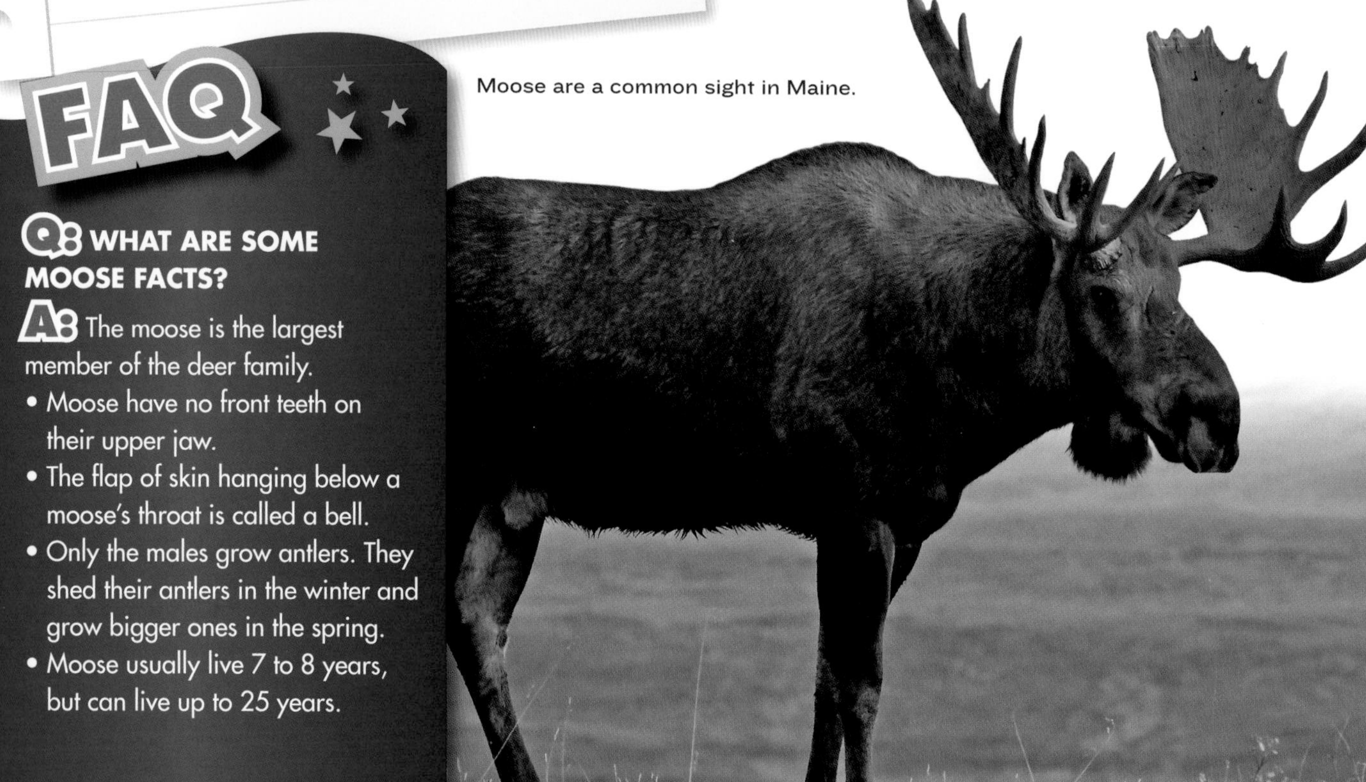
Moose are a common sight in Maine.

This lobster, off the Maine coast near Rockport, has its claws ready in a defensive position.

Near lakes and ponds, you may hear the eerie cackle of the loon. This black-and-white, gooselike waterbird can stay underwater a long time when it dives for fish. Mallards, wood ducks, and herons are also common Maine waterbirds. Black-capped chickadees are Maine's state bird. They flit through the woodlands, along with buntings and grosbeaks. Seabirds such as gulls and terns soar and dive along the coast.

Trout, salmon, and bass are abundant in Maine's rivers and lakes. Offshore, there are saltwater fish such as herring, mackerel, cod, flounder, and tuna. Maine is famous for its lobsters. More lobsters come from the mouth of Penobscot Bay than anywhere else in the world. Crabs, clams, and shrimps are some other Maine shellfish. Boaters often see dolphins and whales out in the ocean. Several kinds of seals live in Maine's waters, too. Colonies of seals gather on the islands and coastal ledges to rest and catch some sleep.

ANDRE THE SEAL

Every spring for more than 20 years, Andre the harbor seal used to show up in Rockland. He came to visit his human friend, a scuba diver named Harry Goodridge. Goodridge had found Andre when the animal was just an orphan pup (baby seal). He taught Andre to do tricks. Soon crowds would gather to watch Andre perform his tricks at feeding time. Word spread about the friendly seal. In time, Andre became famous, capturing hearts around the world,

Goodridge wrote *A Seal Called Andre: The Two Worlds of a Maine Harbor Seal*, and the book inspired a 1994 movie called *Andre*. A life-sized statue of the beloved seal now stands at Rockland Harbor. Andre died in 1986.

ENDANGERED SPECIES

Dozens of Maine animal species have been identified as **endangered** or **threatened**. They may be named on the state list, the national list, or both. Endangered birds include the golden eagle, the roseate tern, and the sedge wren. Several species of whales are among the mammals. Leatherback turtles and box turtles are on the list, too. Several types of fish, including the Atlantic salmon and the shortnose sturgeon, are also endangered.

To help, Maine created the Endangered and Nongame Wildlife Fund in 1983. Citizens can contribute to the fund by purchasing a loon license plate or by checking a box on their state income tax form. That's called the "chickadee check-off" The funds contribute money to support work on Maine's threatened and endangered species!

WORDS TO KNOW

endangered *in danger of becoming extinct*

threatened *likely to become endangered in the foreseeable future*

hydroelectric power *electricity generated by the force of water passing through a dam*

spawn *to lay eggs*

ENVIRONMENTAL ISSUES

Mainers treasure their natural resources. The state's crisp air, sparkling waterways, and lush forests and wetlands make it a wonderful place to live. Over the years, though, human activities have threatened some of these resources. Mainers began a serious environmental movement in the 1960s to help preserve the state's precious resources.

Many efforts have been directed toward the paper industry. This industry has always been important to Maine's economy. However, the paper-bleaching process emits dioxins—chemical substances that cause cancer and other disorders. Some fish absorb dioxins released into the rivers, and humans may take in dioxins by eating fish. Other industrial activities—and even backyard trash burning—can release dioxins into the air and water. By the 1990s, Maine had some of the toughest laws in the country to regulate waste-disposal systems. Accordingly, dioxin levels dropped dramatically.

Dams also became a problem. Many dams were built on Maine's rivers to create **hydroelectric power**. However, some dams were an obstacle for fish. Certain fish species swim upstream to their hatching place every year to **spawn**. But with dams blocking the way, the fish couldn't get upstream. Edwards Dam on the Kennebec River was dismantled in 2000, and others were removed as well. Alongside some dams, people have built fish ladders and fish elevators to move fish past the dams. The alewife ladder in Damariscotta Mills has been in continuous use since 1807.

Tourism is a big part of Maine's economy. Naturally, thousands of people want to visit Maine to enjoy its mountains and coasts. Tourists affect the environment, however. In small towns, the influx of summer visitors strains the waste systems. Emissions from all the cars affect the air quality. New roads, parking lots, and boat launches ruin the landscape, the views, and the peace and quiet. Laws passed since the 1970s have done much to regulate the ways people can alter the environment. Ordinary Mainers have also formed regional groups such as Citizens to Protect the Allagash, a wilderness waterway. And groups such as the Natural Resources Council of Maine continue to push for stronger environmental laws. One and all, they hope to preserve Maine's natural beauty for years to come.

Mainers keep their lakes clean for everyone to enjoy.

MINI-BIO

RACHEL CARSON: ENVIRONMENTALIST

Rachel Carson (1907–1964) was a marine biologist and nature lover. Her 1962 book *Silent Spring* revealed the dangers of DDT (dichloro-diphenyl-trichloroethane), a chemical used to kill plant or animal pests. This book angered the chemical industry but helped launch the environmental movement. Carson did much of the research for her books *The Sea Around Us* and *The Edge of the Sea* near her summer home on Southport Island. The Rachel Carson National Wildlife Refuge, named in her honor, is scattered along 50 miles (80 km) of coast from Kittery to Cape Elizabeth.

Want to know more? See www.fws.gov/northeast/rachelcarson/carsonbio.html

FAQ

Q8 WHAT ARE SOME OF THE FISH SPECIES THAT CAN SWIM UP THE KENNEBEC RIVER NOW THAT EDWARDS DAM IS GONE?

A8 Atlantic salmon, striped bass, shortnose sturgeon, Atlantic sturgeon, American shad, blueback herring, alewife, and rainbow smelt.

READ ABOUT

Penobscot leader Nicholas Andrews wearing the ceremonial attire of his people, 1912

Bone harpoon

8000 BCE
Early people called Paleo-Indians live in what is now Maine

6000 BCE ▲
People of the Archaic culture engage in hunting and sea fishing

4000 BCE
The Red Paint People live in Maine and lands to the north

CHAPTER TWO

FIRST PEOPLE

★

LOOK AT THE PLACE NAMES IN MAINE. You'll find Passamaquoddy, Penobscot, Kennebec, Skowhegan, and Androgscoggin, among others. All are handed down from Maine's original inhabitants. These people were deeply connected to the rivers, forests, and coastal regions of Maine. They named the places in their surroundings, and many of those names remain to this day.

Bark bowl

3500 BCE
Maine's Paleo-Indian population begins to die out

▲ 1000 BCE
People in Maine make pottery and bark objects

1400 CE
Several Wabanaki groups live in what is now Maine

Bone harpoon

EARLY HUMAN CULTURES

By about 10,000 years ago, the first humans known to live in Maine had arrived. Called Paleo-Indians, they hunted large game animals such as caribou and musk ox. Beginning about 8,000 years ago, people of the Archaic culture inhabited Maine. They made stone tools for hunting deer and other wild game. They were also a seagoing people who made boats and spears for fishing.

Around 4000 BCE, the so-called Red Paint People lived in Maine and lands to the north. Their name refers to the bright-red ocher, or iron-oxide powder, found in their burial sites. These people had a seafaring tradition, too, and they hunted swordfish in the ocean. Around 1000 BCE, people in Maine began making ceramic pottery. This tradition continued into modern times. Eventually, Maine's Native people organized themselves into the groups we know today.

Paleo-Indians hunted caribou and other large game animals.

Depiction of a Native American encampment along the coast of Maine

PEOPLE OF THE DAWNLAND

As the first rays of sunlight streamed across the Atlantic Ocean, Wabanakis were the first people to welcome the dawn. Wabanaki is the name given to all the Native Americans of Maine. It means "People of the Dawnland."

By 1400 CE, several Wabanaki groups lived in Maine. They all spoke Agonquian languages and held many of the same beliefs and cultural practices. These groups sometimes fought one another. Eventually they formed an alliance called the Wabanaki Confederacy. As allies, they were better able to defend themselves against the powerful Iroquois who lived nearby.

Today, Maine's four major Native American groups are the Penobscots, Passamaquoddys, Mi'kmaqs, and Maliseets. Collectively, they are still known as Wabanakis. People called Abenakis once lived in Maine, too (their name comes from the same Algonquian word as Wabanaki). However, Abenakis disbanded shortly after European settlers arrived.

Native American Settlements

(Before European Contact)

This map shows the general area of Native American peoples before European settlers arrived.

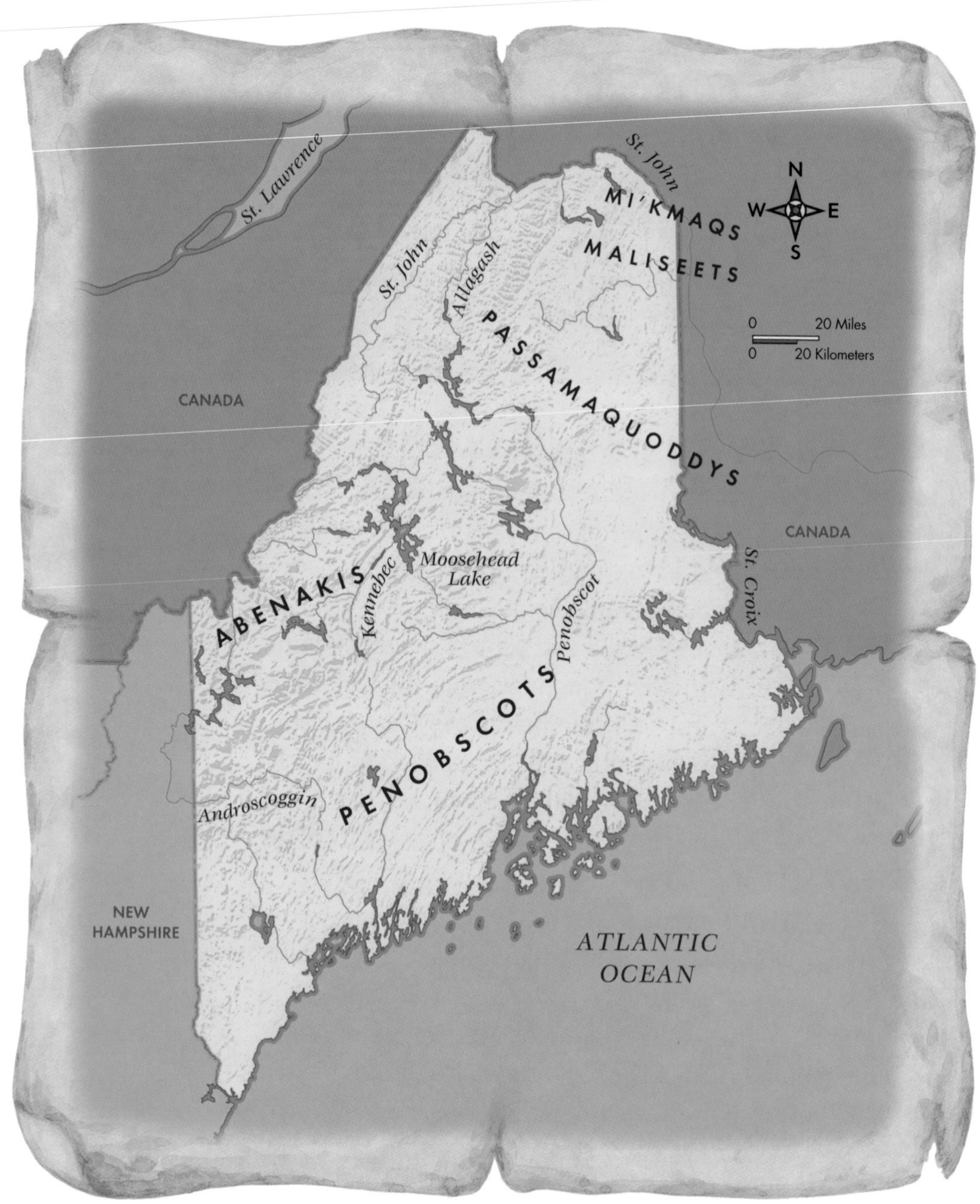

PASSAMAQUODDYS AND PENOBSCOTS

Passamaquoddys and Penobscots lived in eastern Maine. Passamaquoddys ranged from coastal Maine into present-day New Brunswick. Penobscots occupied the lands drained by the Penobscot River and the coastal area near its mouth. These two groups were closely related, and their customs and traditions were very much the same.

In the spring and summer, bands of related families lived in villages of as many as 100 people. They lived in small, round houses called wigwams, which were covered with birch bark. When winter came, families left the village and moved inland to winter camps. Each man had his own hunting ground, which he inherited from his father. All the families returned to the village again in the spring. When traveling overland, people used dogs to carry their gear.

FAQ

Q: WHAT ARE THE ORIGINS OF THE NAMES OF MAINE'S NATIVE AMERICAN GROUPS?

A: Penobscot—comes from *Panawahpskek*, meaning "place where the rocks open out." This was the name of a Penobscot village.

Passamaquoddy—comes from *Peskotomuhkati*, meaning "pollock-spearing place." (Pollock is a fish.)

Mi'kmaq—comes from *nikmak*, meaning "my kin-friends."

Maliseet—means "talks imperfectly" in the Mi'kmaq language. Maliseets call themselves *Wolastoqiyik*, the name for a river in their homeland.

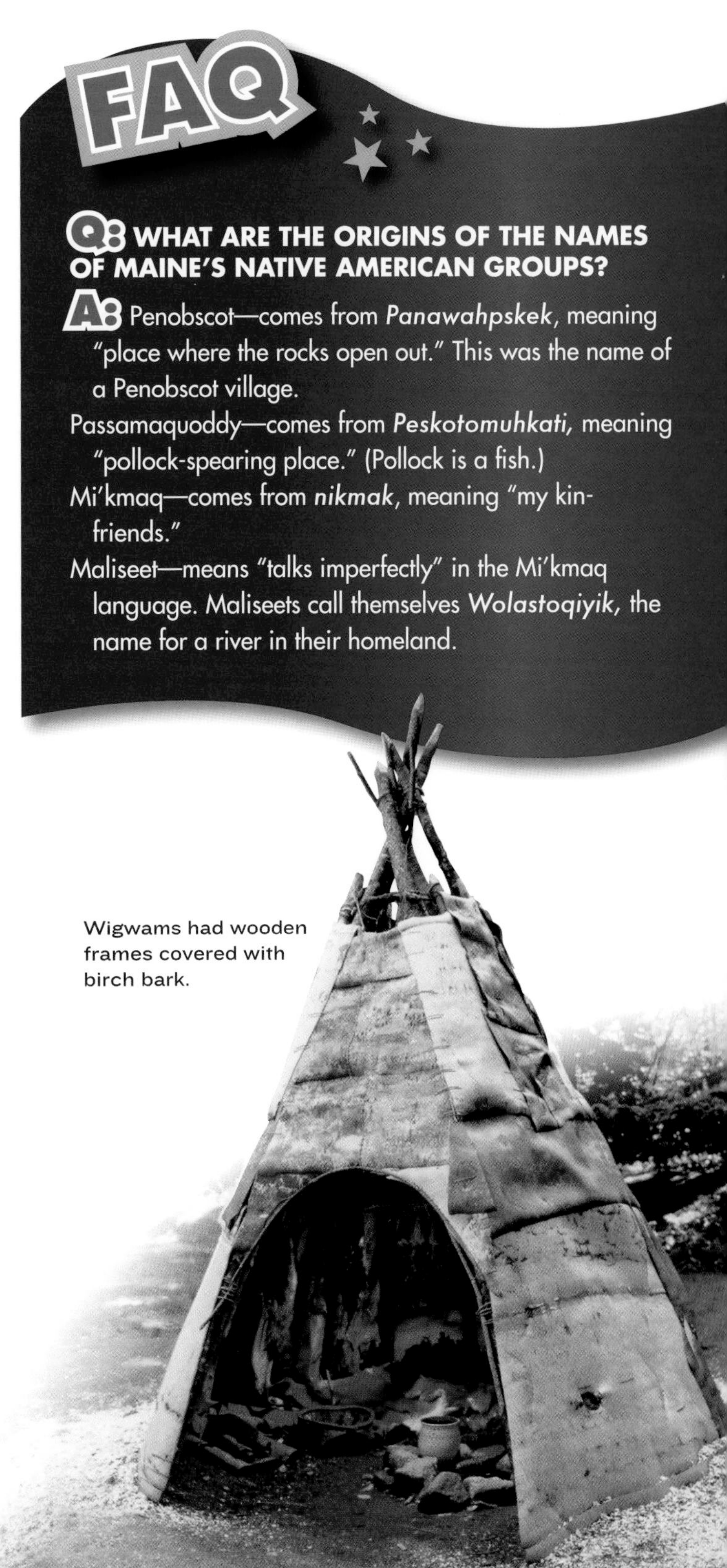

Wigwams had wooden frames covered with birch bark.

SEE IT HERE!

WABANAKI TRADITIONS

Imagine a 3,000-year-old flute made from a swan's bone! That's just one of the 50,000 objects in the collections of the Abbe Museum in Bar Harbor. This museum showcases the history, culture, and lifeways of Maine's Wabanakis. You'll see craft items such as wood carvings, birch bark containers, pottery, and baskets, as well as clothing and tools. Wabanaki legends, beliefs, and customs are highlighted, too.

WORDS TO KNOW

breechcloth *a garment worn by men over their lower body*

resin *clear or light-colored material that is secreted by trees and other plants; used in varnishes, printing inks, and other products*

Daily Life

At the time European settlers began arriving in the 1600s, Penobscot and Passamaquoddy women wore long dresses, and men wore a **breechcloth** and leather leggings. They both wore leather moccasins on their feet, and in the winter they used snowshoes to get through the snow. Penobscots also wore cloaks with pointed hoods. Some chiefs wore a headdress of eagle feathers sticking straight up instead of lying flat.

In the rivers and coastal bays, men caught fish and porpoises using harpoons, pronged fishing spears, and nets. On land, they hunted deer and moose with bows and arrows, spears, and wooden clubs. Expert woodworkers, they carved tree roots into heavy wooden clubs, walking sticks, and tools. They made birch bark canoes using **resin** mixed with charcoal and fat for waterproofing and to seal the joints.

Women cooked and took care of the children. They carried their babies on cradleboards strapped to their backs. Women were the farmers, too. They grew corn, beans, and squash on the fertile coastal plains around the mouths of rivers. They gathered berries and other wild plants to eat and use for medicines.

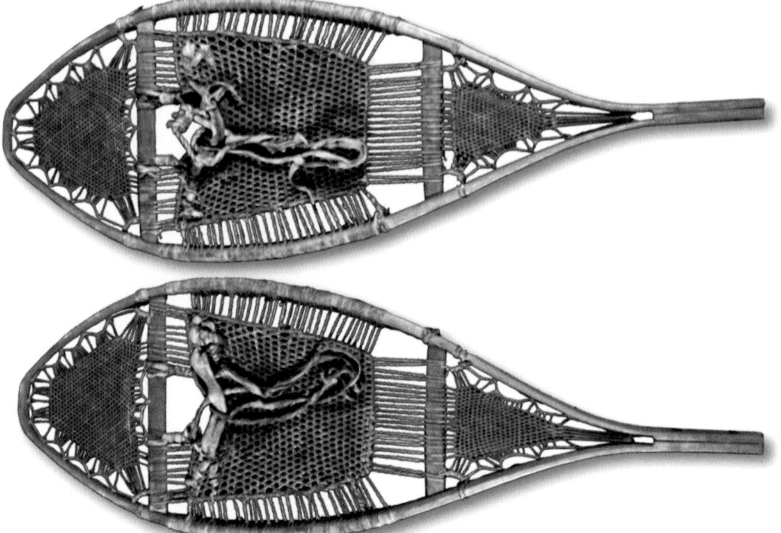

Penobscot snowshoes

Women also wove baskets using bark and grasses. They made baskets in various shapes and sizes depending on their purpose, such as holding potatoes, carrying loads, and storing food. They did quillwork, weaving porcupine quills into leather or bark.

Children and Play

Boys learned to hunt and fish from their fathers. They helped make birch bark canoes and hunted with small bows and arrows. Mothers taught their daughters to cook, farm, gather plants, and weave baskets. Both parents passed on their culture by telling children traditional stories and legends.

Although children worked, they still had time to play. They had favorite toys and games, just as kids do today. Girls played with dolls made out of cornhusks. Another toy was a triangular piece of wood with a hole in the center. Tied to one corner was a ball on a string. The object was to toss the ball up and make it come down through the hole.

A bowl-and-dice game was popular among Penobscots. Sometimes an entire village

Picture Yourself . . .

Building a Birch Bark Canoe

Maine's Wabanakis made birch bark canoes. These canoes were sturdy enough to carry heavy loads, yet light enough for one person to paddle. Parents passed canoe-building skills on to their children. As a Wabanaki child, you knew canoes were made from the bark of the white birch tree. You harvested the bark in the winter, before the sap began running in the spring.

First, you would cut through the bark high on the tree, making a circular cut all the way around the trunk. Then you'd make the same kind of cut near the base of the tree. Finally, you made a third cut running vertically between the high and low cuts. Carefully, you'd peel the bark away, using wooden wedges to separate it from the trunk.

Back at camp, you unrolled the bark and flattened it on the ground. On top of that, you built a frame out of cedar wood. The frame consisted of ribs to hold the canoe in shape, as well as strips to form the upper edges of the canoe. Each piece of cedar was cut, then soaked in water to soften it, then bent into shape and allowed to dry. Finally, you'd bend the birch bark around the frame and attach it in place. You used spruce gum—the sap from a spruce tree—to seal the seams and make the canoe waterproof. As a final touch, you might scrape a design or drawing onto the outside of the canoe.

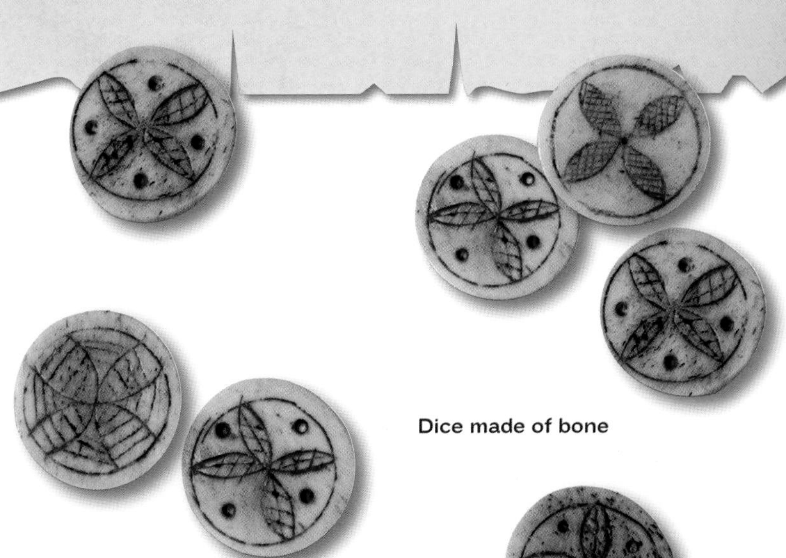

Dice made of bone

played against another village. It was played with a wooden bowl and five or six dice carved from bone or deer antlers. Players cast the dice and tried to win counting sticks from their opponents.

Passamaquoddy boys played a ball-kicking game. They also enjoyed the bundle-and-pin game. It involved a strip of moose hide with holes punched in it. To that was tied a bundle of twigs and a sharp, pointed stick. The object was to toss the moose hide up and spear a hole with the stick.

MI'KMAQS

Mi'kmaqs, or Micmacs, lived in northeastern Maine, extending into Canada. Today, most Mi'kmaq people live in Canada. Like other Wabanaki people, Mi'kmaqs made birch bark canoes. However, Mi'kmaq canoes had a distinctive style, with the sides curving upward in the middle. These lightweight canoes could go up rivers as well as out to sea. In the winter, Mi'kmaqs traveled on sleds. In fact, the word *toboggan* comes from the Mi'kmaq word for "sled."

Mi'kmaq houses were called *wikuom*, the origin of the word *wigwam*. They were made of spruce poles covered with sheets of birch bark. Both men and women wore leather leggings and long robes of skin or fur wrapped around the body. Babies were wrapped in fox or goose skin and carried in cradleboards.

This Mi'kmaq canoe is made of birch bark and was used to travel on rivers and the sea.

A Mi'kmaq box made of birch bark and quills

The Mi'kmaq did not farm. They lived along the seacoast for much of the year. There they harpooned sturgeon, porpoises, seals, walruses, and whales. Other food sources were lobster, squid, and shellfish, as well as salmon and seabirds and their eggs. In the winter, they moved inland, where they hunted large game animals such as moose and caribou. Meat was dried and smoked to preserve it. Roots, berries, and other wild plants added to their diet.

Storytelling was a favorite pastime for Mi'kmaqs. Storytelling get-togethers could last for days, with plenty of singing, dancing, and feasting. Mi'kmaqs enjoyed a dice game, ball-and-stick games, and contests for running, shooting, and wrestling. Mi'kmaq women were known for their quillwork. They wove porcupine quills into beautiful designs on birch bark. Quillwork became a prized craft item to later European settlers.

MALISEETS

Maliseets lived along the St. John River, on what is now the border between Maine and New Brunswick. Today, most Maliseet people live in Canada. Maliseets

LEADER OF A GREAT NATION

Bessabez (?–1615) was a powerful Wabanaki leader who ruled over a nation of 22 villages in central and western Maine. It's believed that he controlled the fur trade between Europeans and Indians in that area. French explorer Samuel de Champlain reported that Bessabez welcomed him with great ceremony. He fed the Frenchmen venison and other wild game and agreed to provide them with beaver skins. Bessabez and Champlain worked together to benefit their people until Bessabez's death in 1615.

WOW

Mi'kmaqs played a ball-and-stick game that is believed to be the origin of hockey.

GLOOSKAP AND THE CHILDREN OF LIGHT

Glooskap, according to Wabanaki tradition, is the creator, a teacher, and a hero. Tales passed on for generations tell about how Glooskap created the earth. He grew lonely, however, so he shot his arrow into an ash tree, and out sprang the Wabanaki people. He called them the Children of Light, or People of the Dawnland, for they were the first to see the sunrise.

Then Glooskap taught his people the skills they needed to live. He taught them how to hunt, fish, and build canoes. He showed them which plants they could eat, and he taught them the names of the stars. Many other traditional stories tell about Glooskap's magical and heroic deeds.

were closely related to Passamaquoddys. In fact, they spoke different versions of the same language and could easily understand each other.

Living near the river, Maliseets were experts at fishing. They also hunted deer, moose, and other wild game. As in other groups, the men hunted and fished, while the women farmed. They raised and harvested corn and gathered berries and other wild plant foods.

ABENAKIS

Abenakis lived in western Maine, west of the Kennebec River. Abenaki people also lived in what are now New Hampshire, Vermont, and Canada. In the winter, they hunted and trapped wild game. In the spring and summer, they fished and farmed along the coast and in

Native Americans using spears to catch salmon

BELOVED HEALER

Molly Ockett (c. 1740–1816) was a beloved Abenaki healer. Her Native name was Singing Bird. She traveled around western Maine, camping near various white settlements. Bethel, Andover, Fryeburg, Paris, and many other towns claimed her as a resident. She treated sick and wounded white settlers wherever she went. For her services, she never took more than one penny. Below is a birch bark box she made for one of her patients. She was buried in Andover, and Bethel celebrates Molly Ockett Day every year.

Birch bark box made by Molly Ockett

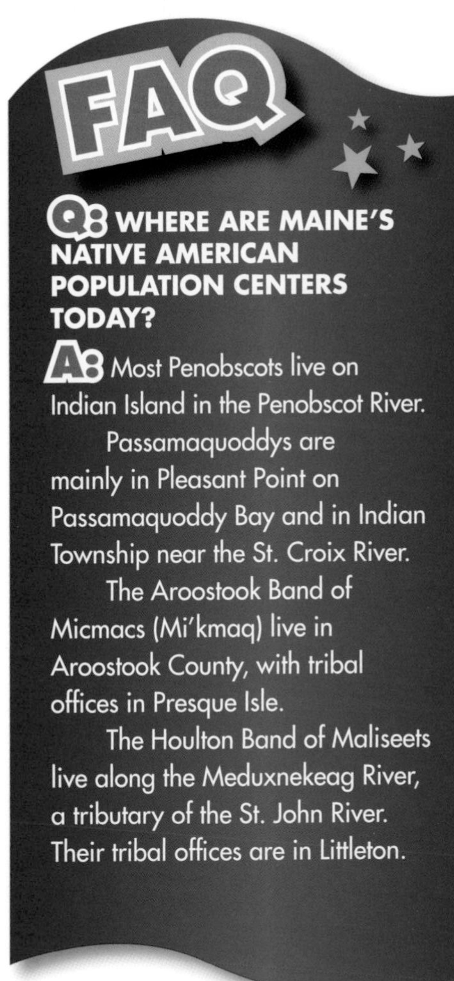

FAQ

Q8 WHERE ARE MAINE'S NATIVE AMERICAN POPULATION CENTERS TODAY?

A8 Most Penobscots live on Indian Island in the Penobscot River.

Passamaquoddys are mainly in Pleasant Point on Passamaquoddy Bay and in Indian Township near the St. Croix River.

The Aroostook Band of Micmacs (Mi'kmaq) live in Aroostook County, with tribal offices in Presque Isle.

The Houlton Band of Maliseets live along the Meduxnekeag River, a tributary of the St. John River. Their tribal offices are in Littleton.

the fertile river valleys. Their farming tools were hoes made from clam shells and shovels made of wood or moose antlers.

Abenaki women ground corn and wheat grains on large, flat rocks, using a heavy pounding stone hung from a flexible branch. Abenakis were also known as healers, possessing great wisdom about **medicinal herbs**.

For Maine's Native Americans, life would change forever when European settlers arrived. Tens of thousands died from diseases they caught from the settlers. Many more were killed while tryhing to protect their homelands. The homelands themselves were eventually taken over by the newcomers.

WORD TO KNOW

medicinal herbs *wild plants used to cure various ailments*

READ ABOUT

Explorer John Cabot may have reached the Maine coast as early as 1498.

1524
Giovanni da Verrazzano reaches what is now Maine

1604
Samuel de Champlain and Pierre du Guast, Sieur de Monts, establish Maine's first colony on St. Croix Island

▲ 1675–1676
King Philip's War is fought

EXPLORATION AND SETTLEMENT

★

WHO WERE THE FIRST EUROPEAN PEOPLE TO REACH MAINE? Around 1100 CE, Norse explorer Leif Eriksson sailed across the Atlantic Ocean to North America. He and his Viking crew made settlements in today's Newfoundland, Canada. Some historians believe Eriksson may have reached Maine, too. In 1498, Italian navigator John Cabot (sailing for England) may have reached the coast of Maine. Because of Cabot's explorations, England claimed present-day Maine.

1720
William Black, a free black man, settles on Bailey Island

▲1765
Falmouth residents protest the stamp tax

1775
The first naval battle of the Revolutionary War takes place off the coast of Machias

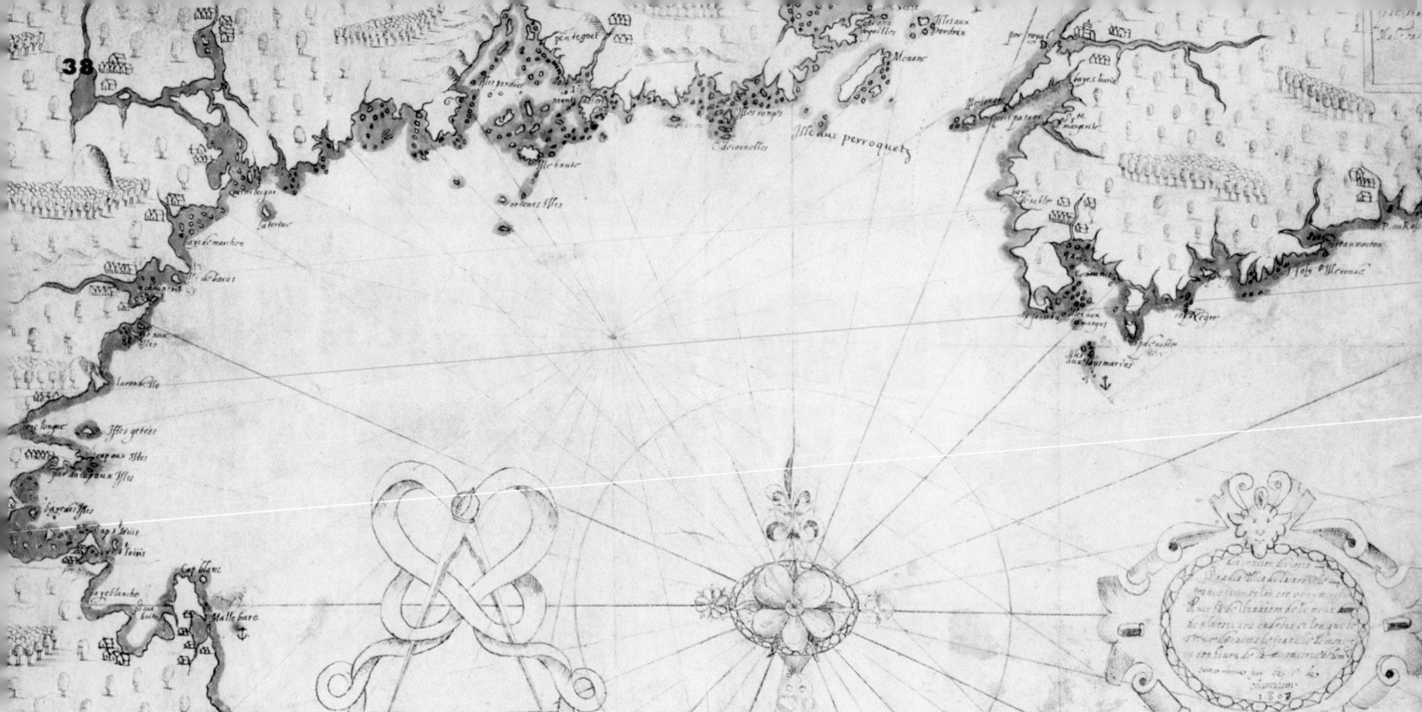

This map was created by explorer Samuel de Champlain in 1607. It shows what is now the East Coast of the United States and the Canadian provinces of New Brunswick and Nova Scotia.

FRENCH EXPLORATIONS

Giovanni da Verrazzano was the first European explorer who definitely reached Maine. Sailing in the service of France, he went ashore on the coast of Maine in 1524. Other European ships arrived over the next century, either on fishing expeditions or to repair their ships.

In 1604, two French explorers—Samuel de Champlain and Pierre du Guast, Sieur de Monts—founded a settlement on St. Croix Island, near the mouth of the St. Croix River. This island—and all of Maine—became part of a territory the French named Acadia. The St. Croix settlement was a disaster, though. Almost half of the French settlers, called Acadians, died of hunger and disease over the harsh winter. The survivors left in 1605.

Champlain discovered an island with tall, treeless peaks. "The mountain summits are all bare and rocky," he wrote. "I name it Isles des Monts Desert." That's French for "island of barren mountains." This island is now Mount Desert (pronounced "dessert") Island.

European Exploration of Maine

The colored arrows on this map show the routes taken by explorers between 1497 and 1605.

Q8 WAS THE POPHAM COLONY THE FIRST ENGLISH SETTLEMENT IN NORTH AMERICA?

A8 Not quite. In 1607, English colonists settled in Popham and in Jamestown, Virginia. The Popham Colony closed down, but the Jamestown colony lasted. Thus, Jamestown is remembered as the first permanent English settlement in the future United States.

ENGLISH COLONISTS

England sent colonizers to the region, too. In 1607, a group called the Plymouth Company established the Popham Colony at present-day Popham. They, like the French colonists, hoped to stay, but during the late summer of 1608, they left, mainly for political and economic reasons.

More English colonists settled along Maine's coast in the 1620s. Many of them abandoned their settlements because of harsh weather and lack of food. Since they occupied Native American lands, they also faced Indian resistance. In 1622, the Plymouth Counsel for New England gave Sir Ferdinando Gorges and Captain John Mason the right to establish the Province of Maine. Gorges and Mason agreed to split this land in 1629. Mason called his portion New Hampshire, while Gorges got much of today's eastern Maine.

Further land grants gave various portions of Maine to other colonists. In the 1650s, the neighboring Massachusetts Bay Colony forcibly took over several Maine settlements. Eager for more land, Massachusetts pushed to get the rest of Maine. The Gorges family protested, but in the end, they sold their land to Massachusetts in 1677. Maine would remain part of Massachusetts until 1820.

Early Maine settlers drying and salting fish

A confrontation between Native Americans and colonists during King Philip's War

INDIAN WARS

Imagine watching strangers take over your town, your playgrounds, your neighborhood, and even your home and yard. That's what it was like for Maine's Native Americans when European settlers arrived. Wabanakis were perfectly willing to **negotiate** with the newcomers. They signed treaties assigning some lands to Indians and other lands to settlers. But when these agreements proved inconvenient, the European settlers just ignored them.

Throughout New England, Indians fought to keep their homelands. Their battles with the Europeans lasted almost 100 years. King Philip's War (1675–1676) was the first major Indian war in the United States. It began in Rhode Island and soon spread northward into Maine.

At the same time, French explorers, fur trappers, and settlers were moving in to what is now Maine. The French not only claimed this area but encouraged Native Americans to attack English settlements. One conflict after another led to the French and Indian War (1754–1763). Actually, Indians fought on both sides of this conflict. In the end, Great Britain was victorious. Then Canada and Maine became British territories.

WORDS TO KNOW

negotiate *to discuss an issue in order to come to an agreement*

A teapot showing a protest of unfair taxes

After the war, Penobscots and Passamaquoddys were confined to a few towns in eastern Maine. Most Mi'kmaq and Maliseet people, forced from their homelands, moved to Canada.

Meanwhile, more and more European colonists settled in Maine. Through land development companies, Massachusetts offered cheap land to any family that would settle in what it called the Maine wilderness. This lured hundreds of farmers into Maine. In the 1740s, landowner Samuel Waldo recruited about 40 German families to settle in Maine. They founded Waldoboro around 1749.

THE REVOLUTIONARY WAR

Life under British rule was not always pleasant. Great Britain needed money to carry on its wars. A simple way to get that money was to tax the colonists. By the 1700s, 13 British colonies were thriving along the Atlantic coast. Most of the colonists' everyday supplies came in on British merchant ships. Britain began charging the colonists high taxes on tea, sugar, and other **staples**. But the Stamp Tax was the last straw. It required colonists to buy tax stamps on newspapers, playing cards, legal documents, and many other items.

Enraged colonists began to attack the tax collectors. In 1765, an angry Maine mob seized tax stamps in Falmouth (present-day Portland). In 1773, colonists in Boston, Massachusetts, boarded a British ship and dumped its **cargo** of tea into the sea. This was called the Boston Tea Party. The next year, Mainers staged a "tea party" of their own. They burned a shipment of British tea in York.

WORDS TO KNOW

staples *essential foods and other supplies*

cargo *trade goods carried on a ship or other vehicle*

At this rate, war was bound to break out—and it did. The first shots of the Revolutionary War (1775–1783) rang out in Lexington and Concord, Massachusetts. Hundreds of Mainers joined in the fight for freedom from Great Britain.

MAINE FIGHTS FOR FREEDOM

With its long coastline, Maine faced attacks from the sea. In 1775, British warships bombarded and burned Falmouth. They wanted to punish the town for refusing to resupply the British navy. In June 1775, a rebel force captured the British ship *Margaretta* off the coast of Machias. This was the first naval battle of the Revolutionary War.

Picture Yourself . . .
as a Revolutionary War Powder Monkey

Bright flashes of cannon fire explode in the night. The sea is pitching your ship from side to side, and the deck is slippery. But you must keep your footing—and run! This was the dangerous life of nine-year-old John Barry of Maine. He served on a warship commanded by Revolutionary War hero John Paul Jones.

Many young boys served as soldiers or sailors in the war. Some were drummer boys and fife players who kept up lively tunes for soldiers on the march. But many—like John Barry—actually served in combat.

Young John worked as a "powder monkey." His job was to scurry down into the cramped storage area belowdecks, fetch gunpowder, and rush it up to the cannons. Small boys like John were preferred because they could easily fit into the storage compartments. John had to be fast and fearless, too. Battles could be won or lost depending on a steady supply of gunpowder. And John had to keep up his courage regardless of the turmoil around him.

Did girls ever work as powder monkeys? Maybe they did. There are tales of girls in the 1700s who disguised themselves as boys and went to sea!

The town of Falmouth was attacked by British forces in 1775.

Benedict Arnold leading an expedition through the Maine wilderness on the way to attack Quebec

Q8 WHAT BECAME OF BENEDICT ARNOLD?

A8 At first, Benedict Arnold was a Revolutionary War hero, considered clever and brave. But he became angry about the way Congress was handling the war. Congress would not pay his wartime expenses or promote him to a higher rank. In 1780, Arnold was caught giving secret American plans to the British. Although he was branded a traitor, he was never captured or punished. He went on to fight on the British side.

Later that year, Maine troops, among others, followed Colonel Benedict Arnold into Canada. He hoped to capture Quebec, but the expedition failed. Another failure took place in 1779. British forces had captured a fort at Castine, on Penobscot Bay, and colonists hoped to win it back. After a fierce naval battle, they were forced to withdraw in defeat.

In 1783, the war ended in victory for the colonial forces. The 13 colonies soon became a new, independent nation—the United States of America! Mainers had finally gained freedom from Great Britain. Next, they would seek freedom from Massachusetts.

Though slavery never played a significant role in Maine, it was not abolished until 1783. Massachusetts abolished slavery that year, and Maine was part of Massachusetts at the time. Among Maine's early settlers were a number of African Americans who served on whaling ships. William Black, a frontiersman and trader from Kittery, was a freed slave. He settled on Bailey Island around 1720. In 1794, Benjamin Darling, a former slave, purchased Horse Island (now Harbor Island). Darling, his white wife, and their two sons became the island's first residents. In 1847, they sold Horse Island and moved to Malaga Island.

The Darlings established Malaga Island as a safe haven for blacks, Native Americans, and poor whites such as Irish, Scottish, and Portuguese immigrants. Its people survived by fishing and farming, lived together peacefully, and intermarried. The island became a multicultural refuge.

Between 1740 and 1784, Maine's population grew from 12,000 to 56,000 people!

These students attended a school on Malaga Island.

READ ABOUT

The forests of Maine supported a healthy logging industry.

1820

Maine becomes the 23rd state

1839

Maine declares war on Great Britain over a border dispute with Canada

1842

The boundary line between Maine and Canada is settled

GROWTH AND CHANGE

★

AFTER THE REVOLUTIONARY WAR, MAINERS CARRIED ON WITH THEIR LIVES. Settlers in the frontier farmed, fished, and cut lumber in the dense northern woods. Maine's luxurious pine forests became the mainstay of its economy. Not only was the wood used in shipbuilding, but it was Maine's leading export.

1852
Harriet Beecher Stowe publishes Uncle Tom's Cabin *while living in Brunswick*

1884
The Bath Iron Works opens in Bath

1894 ▲
The Bangor and Aroostook Railroad begins running

STATEHOOD

Mainers living in the backwoods disliked being ruled by officials in faraway Boston, the capital of Massachusetts. However, they had little say in the matter. Prosperous merchants along the coast were Maine's political leaders. Their sturdy sailing ships brought goods in and out of Maine's harbors. They did business with Boston merchants, and they had no problem being part of Massachusetts.

Maine's ties with Massachusetts would change after the War of 1812 (1812–1815). Americans declared this war on Great Britain because British ships were kidnapping American sailors on the high seas and forcing them to serve in the British navy.

During the war, British troops occupied Penobscot Bay and the entire coast east of the bay. Mainers were panicked and appealed to Massachusetts for protection. But no assistance ever came. Was Massachusetts unable to help? Or did Massachusetts not really care about its frontier district? No one knew. But after the war, even Maine's merchants wanted to separate from Massachusetts to create the state of Maine.

On September 5, 1813, the U.S. ship *Enterprise* and the British ship *Boxer* battled near Monhegan Island, resulting in the *Boxer*'s surrender.

Maine: From Territory to Statehood

This map shows the original Maine territory and the area (in yellow) that became the state of Maine in 1820.

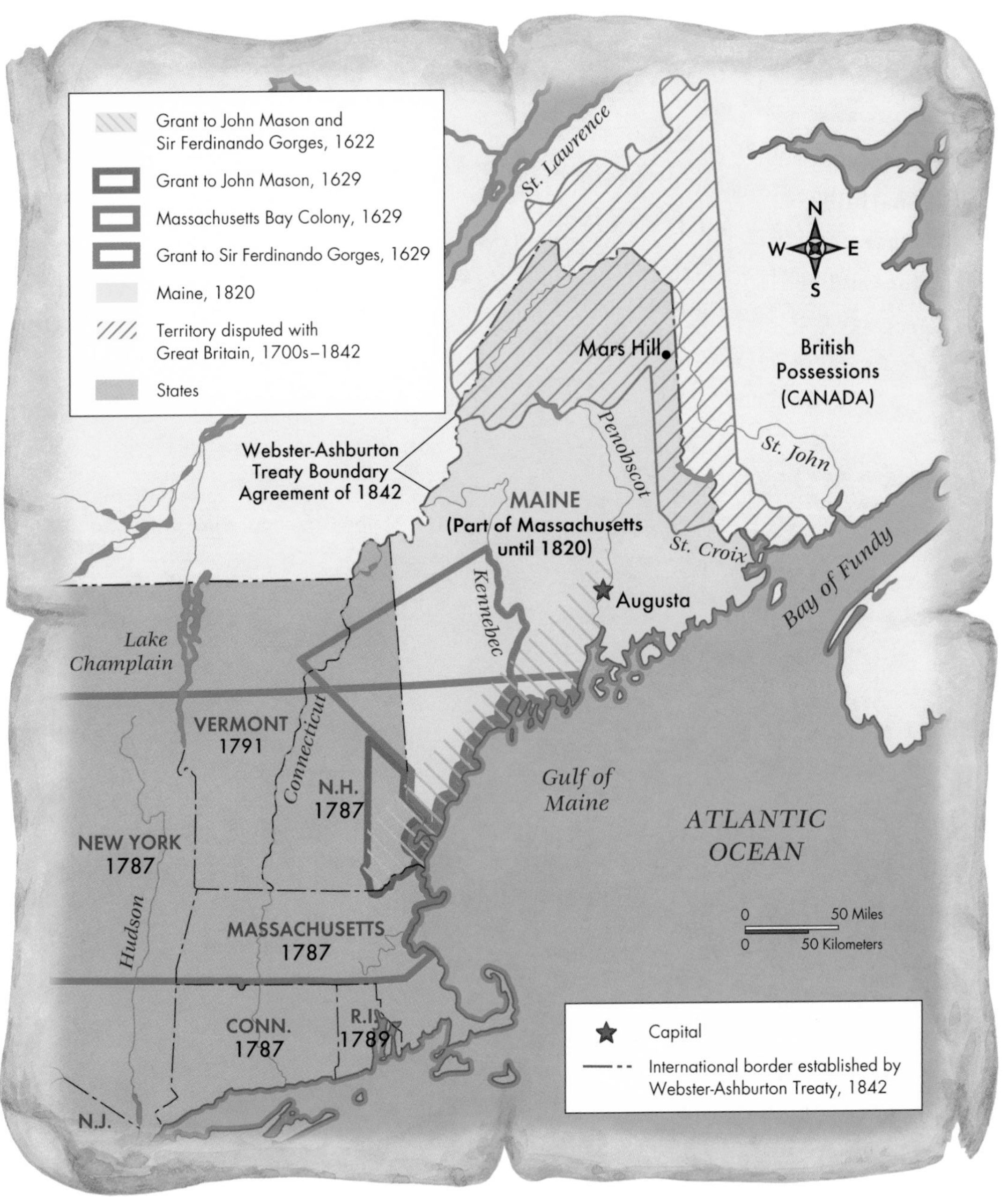

MINI-BIO

WILLIAM KING: THE SULTAN OF BATH

William King (1768–1852) attended school until he was 13. Then he went to work in a sawmill. Eventually, he became a wealthy merchant in Bath and the largest shipowner in Maine. Known as the Sultan of Bath, he also opened the town's first bank. King spent seven years trying to gain Maine's independence from Massachusetts. He served as president of the convention that drew up Maine's first constitution. After statehood in 1820, he became Maine's first governor.

Want to know more? See www.aoc.gov/cc/art/nsh/king_w.cfm

William King and Joseph Treat led the drive for Maine's statehood. Both men had fought in the War of 1812. Under their leadership, Maine drew up a state constitution. Then it appealed to the U.S. Congress for statehood.

The U.S. Congress tried to keep a balance between Slave States and Free States. Finally, in an agreement called the Missouri Compromise, Congress voted to admit Missouri as a Slave State and Maine as a Free State. On March 20, 1820, Maine became the 23rd state in the Union.

The Maine Statehouse in Portland in 1820

THE NORTHEAST BOUNDARY DISPUTE

If Maine was a state, where were its boundaries? This had been a difficult question since the Revolutionary War. The line between Maine and Canada had never been clearly defined. Both Britain and the United States claimed to own the land around the border. Statehood did not resolve the problem. This dispute went on for more than two decades after Maine became a state.

In 1838, some Canadian loggers brought the matter to a head. They cut timber in a part of the Aroostook River valley that American settlers had claimed. Maine sent troops to the area, and Great Britain sent Canadian troops, too. Hostilities increased, and Maine prepared for war.

In 1839, Maine governor John Fairfield declared war on Great Britain. It was the only time in history that a U.S. state declared war on a foreign country. Called the Aroostook War (and nicknamed the Pork and Beans War), it was a bloodless conflict. A **truce** was called before any shots were fired. Finally, the U.S. and British governments resolved the dispute once and for all. In the Webster-Ashburton Treaty of 1842, Maine's northeast boundary was set where it remains today.

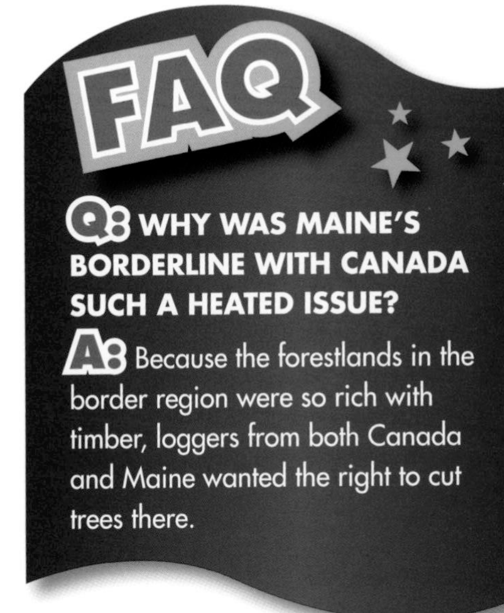

Q8 WHY WAS MAINE'S BORDERLINE WITH CANADA SUCH A HEATED ISSUE?

A8 Because the forestlands in the border region were so rich with timber, loggers from both Canada and Maine wanted the right to cut trees there.

WORD TO KNOW

truce *an agreement to hold off from fighting*

ECONOMIC DEVELOPMENT

You've heard of harvesting crops, but can you imagine harvesting ice? Ice harvesting was a big industry in 19th-century Maine. It involved cutting blocks of ice from frozen rivers and shipping the ice to other cities and countries. A huge icehouse was built on the Kennebec River in the 1820s, and many other icehouses were to follow.

SEE IT HERE!

WANT ICE WITH THAT?

Thompson Ice House was founded in South Bristol in 1826. In just two to three days, 18 to 20 workers there could harvest 8 tons of ice. The ice was shipped as far away as Florida. Now the icehouse is a museum dedicated to the history of Maine's ice industry.

Maine's lumber industry was thriving, too. Water-powered sawmills along the rivers sawed the logs into lumber. That benefited Maine's booming shipbuilding industry. Dozens of towns along the coast had shipyards that built wooden **clipper ships** and other sailing vessels. Portsmouth Naval Shipyard opened in Kittery in 1800. It specialized in building U.S. Navy warships. Fishing was another major coastal industry. Maine's first seafood cannery opened in Eastport in 1842.

WORD TO KNOW

clipper ships *fast sailing ships with tall masts*

Besides sawmills, other types of mills sprang up alongside Maine's rivers. Water-powered factories produced cotton and wool cloth, paper, gunpowder, and other products. Leather goods, such as shoes and boots, were also manufactured. Mining became a booming industry, too. The coastal hills were rich in granite and limestone, and stone quarries employed hundreds of people.

LUMBERING DAYS

"Pine was the prince of the forest," a historian said about Maine's lumbering days. Some might say that lumberjacks were the princes of the forest. Their sheer strength and courage kept a valuable industry alive.

Lumberjacks chopped down the pine trees and dragged the logs to a riverbank. Rivers became highways for transporting logs to sawmills and shipyards. The logs floated for miles down the rushing rivers. At one time, the Penobscot was called the River of Logs. Men called river drivers stood on top of the logs to guide them downstream. Each driver held a long wooden pole with a hook on the end. He used it to keep the logs moving along and to break up logjams.

Logs that went to sawmills were cut into long planks of lumber. Other logs went all the way to coastal shipyards, where hundreds of ships' masts were made from the tall, straight pine trees.

Maine's factories, mills, and workshops needed more workers to fill the available jobs. Fortunately, thousands of immigrants poured into Maine to meet the need for workers. Some were from Ireland, where a potato famine had struck in 1846. In the 1860s, many French Canadians also moved into Maine's mill towns for work.

THE CIVIL WAR

The slavery issue infuriated many Northerners, and some joined the **abolitionist** movement. In 1852, while living in Brunswick, prominent abolitionist Harriet Beecher Stowe published the novel *Uncle Tom's Cabin.* Her goal was to portray the harsh realities of slave life. It captured millions of hearts and minds around the nation at the time and became the best-selling novel of the 1800s.

Hannibal Hamlin was another Maine abolitionist. President Abraham Lincoln chose Hamlin to run as his vice president, and the two carried the 1860 elections. Soon after, the Civil War (1861–1865) broke out. Two generals from Maine—Oliver Otis Howard and Joshua Chamberlain—helped bring victory to the North.

PROFILE OF A PASTOR

In the 1840s, Portland was home to the Reverend Amos Freeman. A pastor of Portland's Abyssinian Meetinghouse from 1841 to 1851, Freeman worked for better employment and education opportunities for blacks. His meetinghouse was both a church and a community center. He was the principal of Portland's school for African American children. He also helped many runaway slaves escape to freedom and became a leading abolitionist voice.

WORD TO KNOW

abolitionist *a person who worked to end slavery*

Joshua Chamberlain led the troops of the 20th Maine at the battle of Gettysburg, Pennsylvania, in July 1863.

MINI-BIO

OLIVER OTIS HOWARD: FOUNDER OF HOWARD UNIVERSITY

Oliver Otis Howard (1830–1909), born in Leeds, was a Civil War general. After the war, he became head of the Freedman's Bureau, an agency to help newly freed slaves. In 1867, he helped found Howard University in Washington, D.C., for African Americans. He served as its president for six years. Howard University's noteworthy graduates include Nobel Prize–winner Toni Morrison, U.S. Supreme Court justice Thurgood Marshall, and UN ambassador Andrew Young.

Want to know more? See www.pbs.org/weta/thewest/people/d_h/howard.htm

INDUSTRIAL GROWTH

Maine's manufacturing industries grew stronger after the Civil War. Rushing rivers turned the wheels that made the factories run. Soon people thought of a new way to use water power: to generate electricity. In the 1890s, Maine built dams and hydroelectric plants on the Androscoggin, Kennebec, Penobscot, Saco, and many other rivers and streams.

Tourists began visiting Maine in the late 1800s. Some preferred the elegant resort hotels along the coast. Others took steamboats upriver to country cottages. The Bangor and Aroostook Railroad began in 1894, and the train made it easy for tour-

In the late 1800s, tourists flocked to the beaches and elegant hotels of Maine.

A crowd waits for the next train at the Bangor and Aroostook Railroad Station in New Sweden.

ists to reach Aroostook County and the northern woods. There they enjoyed fishing, hunting, and hiking by day and nestling by the fire in cozy log cabins at night.

In the late 1800s, the days of wooden shipbuilding were winding down. Steel-hulled ships became the wave of the future. In 1884, Bath Iron Works opened in Bath. It specialized in ships with steel bodies. The U.S. Navy became its biggest customer. In the early 20th century, Portsmouth Naval Shipyard was busy, too. During World War I (1914–1918), it launched the navy's first submarine.

1948 ▲
Margaret Chase Smith becomes the first woman elected to the U.S. Senate

1954 ▲
Edmund Muskie is elected governor

1959
A law barring discrimination by public businesses is passed

CHAPTER FIVE

MORE MODERN TIMES

★

WHEN THE GREAT DEPRESSION STRUCK IN 1929, MANY MAINE FARMS, FACTORIES, AND MILLS CLOSED DOWN. But as Mainers bounced back from the Depression, paper mills became more productive than ever. Factory workers began to form labor unions in the 1930s, too. Through the unions, they were able to get better working conditions and wages.

1972
Gerald Talbot becomes the first African American elected to the state legislature

1980
President Jimmy Carter signs the Indian Land Claims agreement

2003
Maine passes a bill to bring low-cost health insurance to residents by 2009

MINI-BIO

HAZEL SINCLAIR: CREATING A PLACE OF REST

Vacationers have always enjoyed spending summers at Kittery Point. That's where Hazel Sinclair (1902–1995) worked as a maid and cook in the 1930s. During World War II, she worked at Portsmouth Naval Shipyard. She and her husband, Clayton, saw that most Kittery Point hotels weren't open to African Americans. So the couple began renting out rooms in their home to black tourists. They named their bed-and-breakfast establishment Rock Rest. Hazel managed the place and cooked meals using vegetables from her garden.

Want to know more? See www.seacoastnh.com/blackhistory/sinclair.html

WAR AND POSTWAR GROWTH

Maine's economy boomed during World War II (1939–1945). Its factories produced boots and uniforms for U.S. troops. Maine's shipyards built warships, cargo ships, and submarines for the navy, and dozens of navy destroyers were built at Bath Iron Works.

After the war, Maine encouraged new industries to come into the state. New air force bases were established, and several electronics companies opened. Tourism was on the rise, too. New highways, hotels, and ski resorts were built to draw tourists to Maine.

A family camping on Damariscotta Lake in the 1950s

Two Maine political leaders came into the spotlight. One was Margaret Chase Smith. In 1948, she became the first woman elected to the U.S. Senate. The other was Edmund Muskie. For decades, Mainers had supported Republicans. But that changed in 1954 when they elected Muskie, a Democrat, as governor. He went on to serve as a U.S. senator and U.S. secretary of state.

WOW

During the World War II years of 1943 to 1944, Bath Iron Works launched an average of one new navy ship every 17 days!

CIVIL RIGHTS

Like the rest of the nation, Maine was swept up in the civil rights movement of the 1950s and 1960s. Many Mainers began speaking out against racial discrimination. Native Americans overcame unfair laws and were allowed to vote. As early as 1947, African Americans in Portland had formed a branch of the National Association for the Advancement of Colored People (NAACP).

In 1959, Maine passed a law barring public businesses from discriminating against customers based on race, religion, or ancestry. In the 1960s, Portland's NAACP began pushing for a law to prohibit landlords from discriminating against blacks in rental housing, and the Fair Housing Act was passed in 1965. The Maine Human Rights Act of 1971 banned discrimination in a wide range of areas, such as housing, employment, education, and money lending. Gradually, Maine's African Americans gained the rights they deserved. In 1972, Gerald Talbot of Portland became the first African American elected to the state legislature. He had served as president of Portland's NAACP.

These Native Americans in Oldtown cast ballots for the first time in September 1955.

Managing the Fisheries: Will It Work?

PRO

"[The new law] ensures that decisions about fisheries management policy will take local concerns fully into account and provide for local voices to be heard in the management decision making process."

—U.S. Representative Tom Allen of Maine

In December 2006, Congress passed a new law designed to prevent overfishing. It allows local fishing councils, rather than the federal government, to set limits on the amount of fish that can be caught. This would give small, family-owned fishing businesses a voice in regulating their industry.

CON

"[The new law] . . . doesn't expand membership on the regional councils to include more public members; as it currently stands, the council appointees are dominated by the commercial fishing industry."

—*Kennebec Journal*, December 12, 2006

However, some people think that the law does not go far enough. They believe that large fishing companies will control the process and make decisions that benefit themselves rather than small-scale fishers.

SEE IT HERE!

SAVING THE SALMON

Craig Brook National Fish Hatchery is in Orland, northwest of Mount Desert Island. It's devoted to preserving the Atlantic salmon. Each year, the salmon swim up Maine's rivers to spawn. But their numbers are declining as a result of overfishing, pollution, dams, and other factors. The hatchery raises baby salmon and releases them into rivers. In its spawning rooms, you can see salmon eggs and baby salmon, called fry. You'll also learn all about efforts to preserve the Atlantic salmon.

PROTECTING THE ENVIRONMENT

Industry and tourism powered Maine's growth. But Mainers found that growth had a downside. Wastes from cities and factories were polluting the state's waterways. In the 1970s, Maine began passing laws to protect the environment. Some laws called for cleaner water and air. Others were designed to protect wildlife and natural landscapes.

Protecting salmon and other fish became a special focus for environmentalists. Some dams had to be removed so the fish could swim upstream to spawn. Edwards Dam on the

Kennebec River, Columbia Falls Dam on the Pleasant River, and others were dismantled in the 1990s and early 2000s. Special programs were introduced to increase the salmon populations through hatcheries and various fish-moving equipment.

NATIVE AMERICAN LAND CLAIMS

In the 1970s, Maine's Native Americans took a bold step to reclaim the lands that had been taken from them illegally. They said the first violation had occurred in the 1700s. But in the 1960s, illegal seizures were still taking place. The disputed land amounted to about 12.5 million acres (5 million hectares).

MINI-BIO

SAMANTHA SMITH: PEACEMAKER, AGE 10

Ten-year-old Samantha Smith (1972–1985) of Manchester believed in world peace. In 1982, the Soviet Union was building up nuclear weapons. Samantha was concerned that nuclear war might break out. But she didn't just worry about it. She wrote to Soviet president Yuri Andropov, appealing for peace. Andropov, touched by her letter, invited her to tour the Soviet Union. Samantha accepted the offer and became a celebrity for the cause of peace. Sadly, she lost her life in an airplane crash at age 13.

Want to know more? See www.samanthasmith.info

In 1980, President Jimmy Carter signed a bill that returned land to Native Americans in Maine.

To regain their lands, Passamaquoddys filed a lawsuit in 1974. Legal battles dragged on for years against the state of Maine and the U.S. government. Finally, in 1980, the lawsuit was settled. It benefited the Passamaquoddy, Penobscot, and Maliseet people. They were awarded $81.5 million—the largest amount ever granted in an Indian land-claim case.

MAINE TODAY

Maine faces some difficult challenges today. Among them are concerns about protecting the environment while preserving businesses and jobs. One example is the fishing industry. Government regulations aim to preserve the fish population. But some of those rules make it hard for fishers to earn a living. Forestry has had troubles as well. Insects destroyed a huge number of forest trees in the 1970s and 1980s. Heavy cutting reduced the tree supply, too. Both of these situations hurt the paper industry.

Workers from the Portsmouth Naval Shipyard in Kittery march in a successful protest to keep their base open.

Maine welcomes tourism as a major source of income. At the same time, the state is determined to keep its natural areas unspoiled. State leaders are working hard to keep Maine both beautiful and economically sound for future generations.

The closure of military bases threatened to affect Mainers, too. Loring Air Force Base in Presque Isle was closed in 1994. Then in 2005, the U.S. Defense Department announced plans to close or scale back operations at Portsmouth Naval Shipyard in Kittery, Brunswick Naval Air Station, and the Defense Finance and Accounting Center in Limestone. These cutbacks would have put thousands of Mainers out of work. Citizens and state leaders campaigned hard to keep these bases open, and they were partially successful. Portsmouth Naval Shipyard will remain open, and the Limestone center will even expand. Brunswick Naval Air Station is scheduled to close in 2011.

The health of Maine's citizens is another concern. Rising health care costs affect people across the state—and the entire nation. Maine approached this problem by passing a bill in 2000 to lower the cost of prescription drugs. The state passed another health care bill in 2003. It aims to bring low-cost health insurance to all residents by 2009. With a state motto of *Dirigo*, Latin for "I lead," Maine hopes to lead the nation in providing health benefits for its people.

This doctor and patient will both benefit from the health care measures that Maine has passed.

READ ABOUT

Mainers set sail from Boothbay Harbor.

PEOPLE

★

IMAGINE YOU'RE SAILING ALONG THE ATLANTIC COAST. Would you sail "up" to Maine or "down" to Maine? If you lived in the days of sailing ships, when Boston was the king of the seas, you'd sail down! To get from Boston to Maine, seamen used to say they were sailing "down east." That meant eastward and downwind—in the direction the winds blow. Mainers were called Down Easters, and the nickname has stuck to this day, especially for those living along the northern coast. Down Easters are proud of their heritage and the people and cultures that make up their state.

THE WAY LIFE SHOULD BE

Cross into Maine from Portsmouth, New Hampshire, and you're greeted by a sign: "Maine—The Way Life Should Be." All of a sudden, traffic is lighter, and life seems to move at a slower pace. Hundreds of charming towns and fishing villages line the coast. Boats pull into the harbors to unload their lobsters, scallops, or fish from the day's catch.

For people who live along the coast, the sea has a lot to do with their way of life. Summer is a time to watch boat races, dig in the sand for clams, or have a lobster bake on the beach. Strolling along the rocky shores, people hear the waves crash and smell the ocean spray. When evening falls, the fog rolls in, lighthouses twinkle, and foghorns echo through the darkness.

A family enjoys cross-country skiing during a Maine winter.

Go deeper into Maine, away from the coast, and you'll see different lifestyles. In the small towns and rural areas, fall and winter are fun seasons. In autumn, hunters take to the woods. People might catch a wild turkey for Thanksgiving dinner. In winter, some people chop down their own Christmas trees or go cross-country skiing.

The melting winter snow makes for a soggy spring, known as "mud season." In the summer, people emerge from their homes to enjoy the outdoors again.

Where Mainers Live

The colors on this map indicate population density throughout the state. The darker the color, the more people live there.

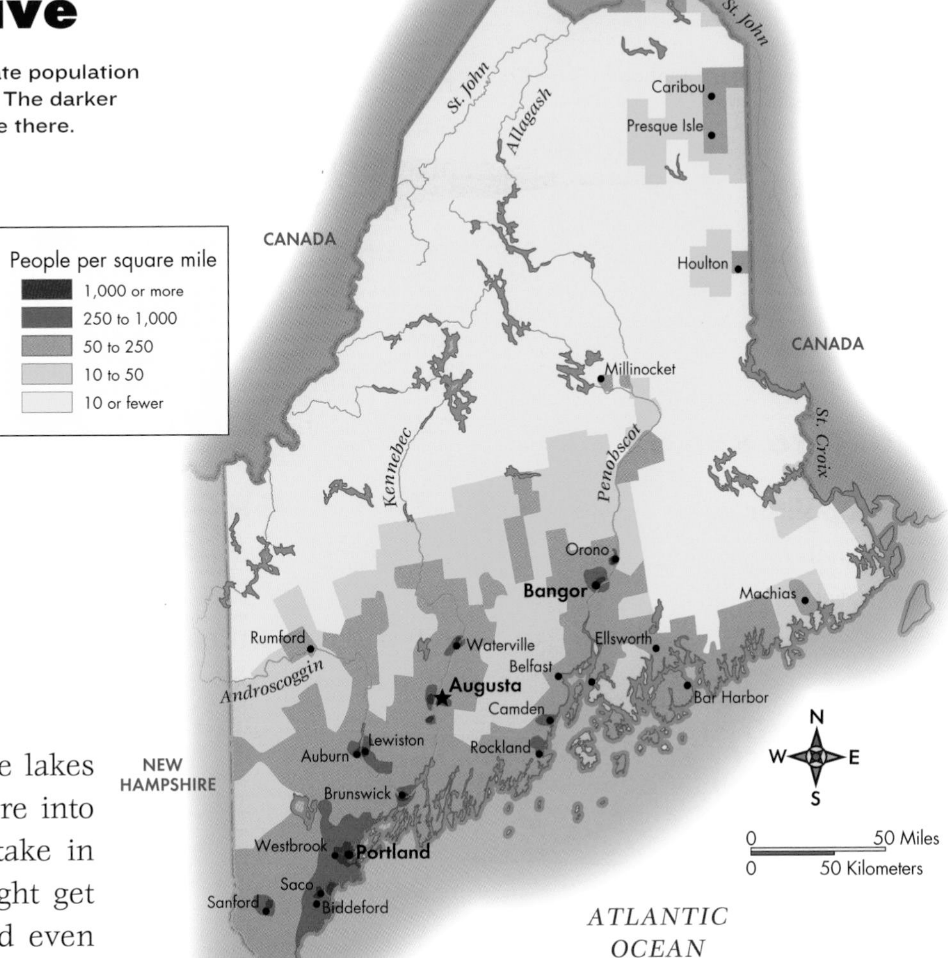

They go fishing in the lakes and streams or venture into the forests. As they take in the scenery, they might get a glimpse of deer and even bears and moose. Wherever they live, Mainers are sure to agree that life in Maine is "The Way Life Should Be."

WHERE PEOPLE LIVE

Maine isn't a gigantic state, and its population isn't huge, either. Among the 50 states, Maine ranks 40th in population. In 2006, the state was home to an estimated 1,321,574 people.

WOW

Six cities in the United States have a larger population than the entire state of Maine! They are New York City; Los Angeles, California; Chicago, Illinois; Houston, Texas; Philadelphia, Pennsylvania; and Phoenix, Arizona.

Big City Life

This list shows the population of Maine's biggest cities

Portland	63,011
Lewiston	35,734
Bangor	31,008
South Portland	23,784
Auburn	23,156

Source: U.S. Census Bureau, 2006 estimates

WORD TO KNOW

metropolitan area *a dense population region that usually includes several towns*

Mainers are not spread out evenly across the state. More than half the population is clustered in the southwestern part of the state. Almost 40 percent of Mainers make their home in the **metropolitan area** of Portland, South Portland, and Biddeford. Maine's largest cities are Portland, Lewiston, Bangor, South Portland, and Auburn. Augusta, the capital, is the ninth-largest city. Its population in 2000 was only 18,560!

Beyond the cities and towns, people are spread out rather thinly. Three out of five Mainers live in rural areas. Only two states—Vermont and West Virginia—have a higher percentage of rural residents.

ETHNIC GROUPS

Parlez vous français? ("Do you speak French?") Lots of Mainers do. Waves of French Canadians arrived in the 1800s. Some settled in the mill towns of central Maine, such as Lewiston and Waterville. Others began farming in the far northern St. John River valley.

People QuickFacts

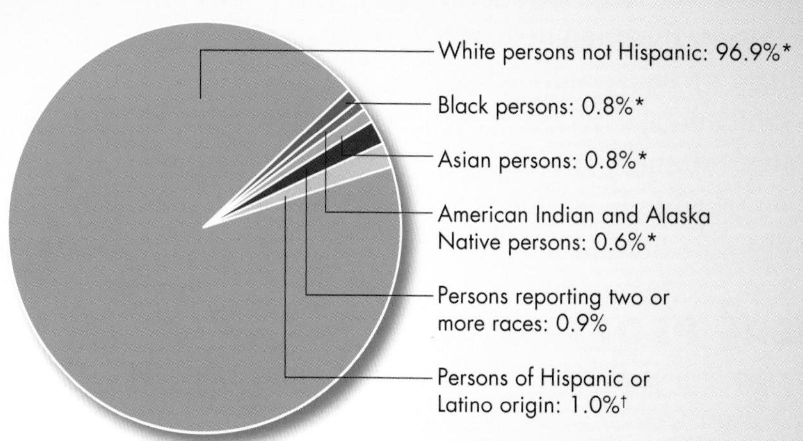

* Includes persons reporting only one race
† Hispanics may be of any race, so they also are included in applicable race categories
Source: U.S. Census Bureau, 2005 estimate

Maine Population Growth

This chart shows Maine's population growth between 1790 and 2000, and it projects that by 2010 there will be almost 1.4 million people living in the state.

Source: U.S. Census Bureau

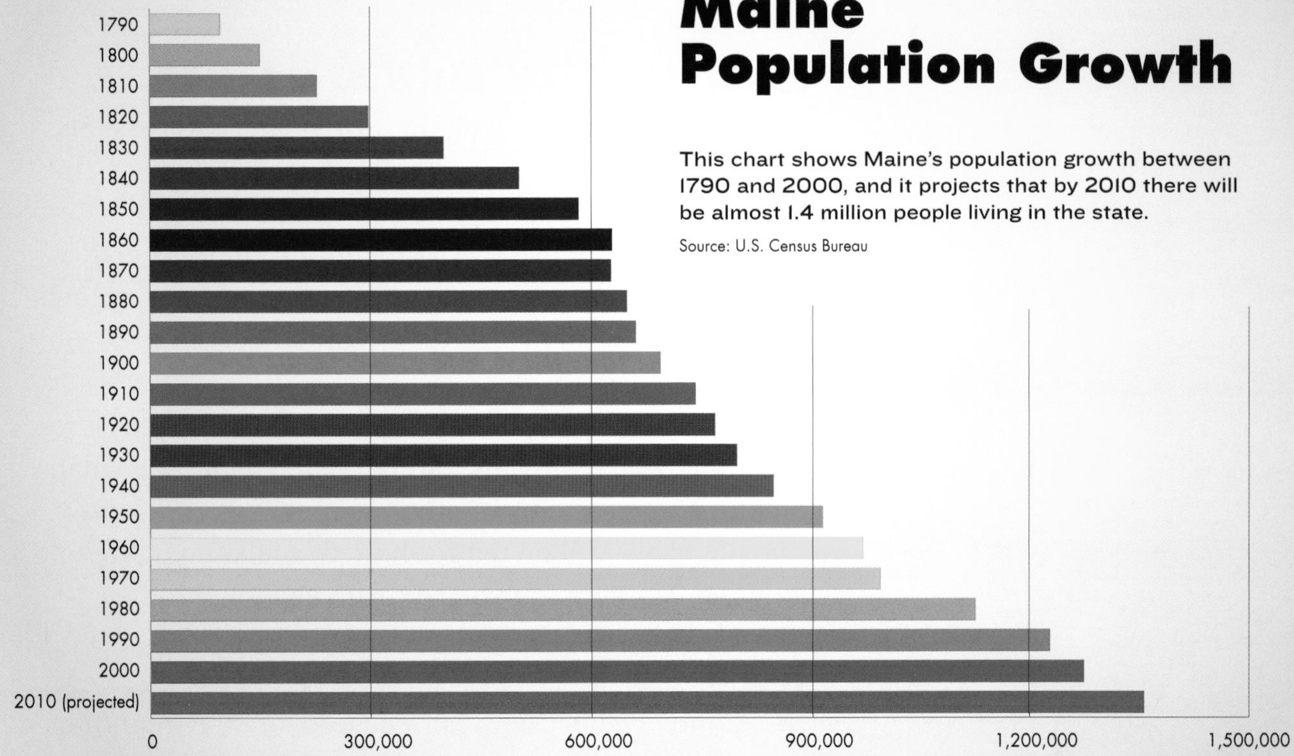

Today, French Canadians are still a large ethnic group in Maine. In the 2000 census, almost 23 percent of Mainers reported French or French Canadian ancestry. In fact, 5.3 percent of Mainers still speak French at home—a higher percentage than in any other state.

About 97 percent of Mainers are descended from Europeans. Their ancestors came from England, France, Ireland, Germany, Italy, and many other countries. But people from all over the world have found new homes in Maine. For example, many people from the war-torn African country of Somalia began settling in Lewiston in 2001. Asian, Hispanic, African American, and Native American people live in Maine, too. Each of these groups makes up 1 percent or less of the total population.

FAQ

Q8 WHAT ARE SOME MAINE TOWNS WITH A STRONG FRENCH-CANADIAN HERITAGE?

A8
- Madawaska
- Frenchville
- St. Agatha
- Lewiston
- Auburn
- Waterville
- Biddeford

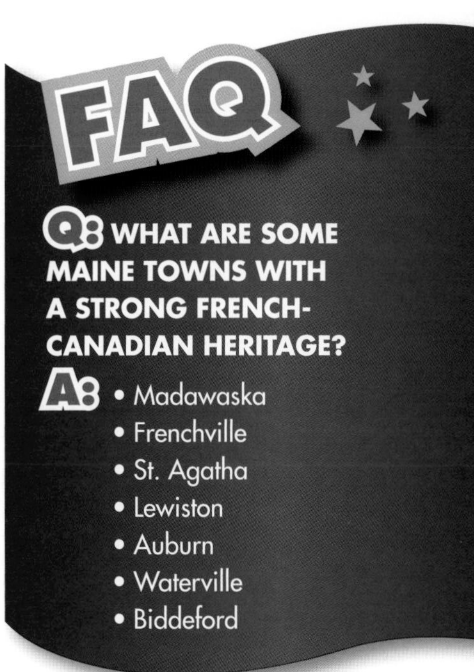

HOW TO TALK LIKE A MAINER

Mainers have some unique words and expressions. *Ayuh* means "You're absolutely right." *Bahmy* is the Maine version of "balmy," which means "warm." But in Maine, people use the words in a humorous way to talk about very cold weather. If someone asks, "How cold was it last night?" the reply might be, "Bahmy—50 degrees below zero."

The dooryard is the area of a yard that's closest to the door. *Gawmy* means "clumsy," and a *dite* is a small amount. *Gorry* means "golly," as in, "By gorry, look at that big fish!" And no matter how you talk, if you're not a native, Mainers say you're "from away"!

HOW TO EAT LIKE A MAINER

In Maine, you'll see fresh seafood on the menu in many restaurants and diners. Freshly caught lobster, clams, and other shellfish are favorites near the coast. On summer evenings, people enjoy going to the beach for a lobster bake. They build a fire and steam lobsters, clams, and corn-on-the-cob in a big pot. Clambakes and clam boils are similar, and they're a fun part of many festivals. Of course, Maine has its own version of clam chowder, too. Maine farmers grow potatoes, blueberries, and beans, and Mainers turn these products into a variety of delicious dishes.

HOW TO EAT A COOKED LOBSTER

- Twist the claws off.
- Crack the big claws with pliers or a nutcracker and pull the meat out with a fork or pick.
- Break the small claws by hand and suck the meat out.
- Twist the tail off the body and push the meat out the open end. This is the tastiest part.
- Bite on the legs to break their shells and nibble the meat out.
- Pull the shell off the body. Then you'll see the tomalley. It's the liver, and it's green. Some people love tomalley, but you may not want to eat it!

MENU

Lobster roll

Lobster roll
A lobster mixture served in a grilled hot dog bun; a fast-food way to eat lobster!

Moxie
A dark, bitter soft drink made in Lisbon, Maine, and popular in the state.

Quahogs
(pronounced KOH hogs) Hard-shell clams. Some Mainers say they're rubbery. Quahogs stuffed with minced meat, onions, bread crumbs, and spices are called stuffies.

Steamers
Soft-shell clams with thin shells that don't completely close.

Yellow eyes
Small, cream-colored beans with a yellowish spot where it was attached to the pod; popularly served as baked beans.

Bean-hole beans
Lumberjacks stayed in camps on their work sites. Their favorite food was bean-hole beans, which were baked in an iron pot buried in the ground. They are still popular in Maine today.

TRY THIS RECIPE
Maine Clam Chowder
Maine clam chowder is made with steamer clams and has a milky broth. New England clam chowder is milky, too, but it's thickened with flour and uses hard-shell clams. Manhattan clam chowder, made with tomatoes, has a red broth. Rhode Island clam chowder has a clear broth. Try out this recipe, but be sure to have a grown-up nearby to help.

Ingredients:

¼ pound salt pork, diced
1½ cups onions, diced
1 quart water
3 cups potatoes, diced
2 cups steamer clams, chopped or ground (fresh clams work best, but canned clams are okay, too)
Salt and pepper
1 12-ounce can evaporated milk
Oyster crackers

Instructions:

Sauté the salt pork and onions in a skillet until the onions are tender. Scrape into a soup kettle. Add the water and bring it to a boil. Add the potatoes and bring it back to a boil. Add the clams. Lower the heat and simmer until the potatoes are softened. Add the salt and pepper to taste. Stir in the evaporated milk. Let it sit a while, and reheat before serving. Put oyster crackers into your chowder before eating. Makes about 4 servings.

Lobster and corn-on-the-cob

GETTING AN EDUCATION

Be glad you didn't live in Kennebunk in the 1700s. According to legend, your schoolhouse would have been a vacant log sheep pen with no windows and no doors. How did the students get in? They had to climb into the end of the pen through a small open space beneath the roof. Then they had to jump down to the floor!

Schools in Maine have come a long way since then. In 1800, Maine had only seven schools that we would call high schools today. These town-supported schools prepared students for university study. In 1828, Maine established state-supported public schools. Today, more than 200,000 students from kindergarten through 12th grade attend Maine schools. About 1 out of 12 students attends a private school. Young Mainers are required to attend school from ages 7 through 17.

Maine's first college was Bowdoin College, founded in Brunswick in 1794. Bates College was founded by abolitionists in 1855 and was the first coeducational college in New England. Today, these schools are just two of Maine's many private colleges and universities. The state-supported University of Maine is the state's largest university. It has seven branches throughout the state. Another college, the Maine Maritime Academy in Castine, teaches all aspects of seamanship.

FAQ

Q8 WHO ARE SOME FAMOUS GRADUATES OF BOWDOIN COLLEGE?

A8
- Franklin Pierce, 14th U.S. president
- Nathaniel Hawthorne, author
- Henry Wadsworth Longfellow, poet
- Oliver Otis Howard, founder of Howard University
- Robert E. Peary, Arctic explorer

Students form a human pyramid at Bowdoin College.

Writer Stephen King writes novels about mystery and horror.

MINI-BIO

BARRY DANA: PRESERVING THE ANCIENT WAYS

As a child, Barry Dana (1959–) learned to love the old ways of the Penobscot people. His grandparents told him traditional stories and taught him to respect the natural world. As an adult, Dana served several years as tribal chief of the Penobscot Nation. He fought hard to clean up pollution in the Penobscot River, a sacred waterway for his people. He also worked to keep the Penobscot language alive by teaching it to children at Indian Island School.

Want to know more? See www.penobscotnation.org/Articles/072201.htm

MAINE WRITERS AND STORY LOCATIONS

Maine is the birthplace of three great American poets—Henry Wadsworth Longfellow (1807–1882), Edwin Arlington Robinson (1869–1935), and Edna St. Vincent Millay (1892–1950). Sarah Orne Jewett (1849–1909) was a novelist whose stories take place in the seaside region around South Berwick, where she lived. Today, Maine's most famous living author is Stephen King (1947–). Many of his scary novels have been made into movies.

MINI-BIO

HENRY WADSWORTH LONGFELLOW: TELLING HISTORY IN VERSE

Henry Wadsworth Longfellow (1807–1882) is one of the nation's best-loved poets. His poems have a flowing rhythm, making them easy to memorize. Longfellow's works include *The Song of Hiawatha*, *Paul Revere's Ride*, *Evangeline*, and *The Courtship of Miles Standish*. They present romantic versions of events in early U.S. history. Longfellow was born in Portland. He attended Bowdoin College and later taught there. His childhood home, the Wadsworth-Longfellow House in Portland, is now a museum.

Want to know more? See www.hwlongfellow.org/

Many beloved children's book authors have had strong ties to Maine, too. One is E. B. White, author of *Charlotte's Web* and *Stuart Little*. Although he was from New York, he spent summers in Maine before moving there in 1953. Another is Robert McCloskey, who also spent his summers in Maine. He wrote and illustrated *Blueberries for Sal*, *Make Way for Ducklings*, *One Morning in Maine*, and other kids' books. Lea Wait grew up in Maine. Her young adult novels such as *Wintering Well*, *Seaward Born*, and *Stopping to Home* are set in Maine in the 1800s.

Author E. B. White near his home in Maine

Maine is the chosen setting for many other popular novels for young people. Among them are Gary Schmidt's *Lizzie Bright and the Buckminster Boy*, Dan Gutman's *The Get Rich Quick Club*, and Mary Downing Hahn's *Look for Me by Moonlight* and *Deep and Dark and Dangerous*. Kate Douglas Wiggin's *Rebecca of Sunnybrook Farm* is a favorite classic set in Maine.

The Maine State Library encourages good children's literature. Every year, its Youth Services Section presents the Lupine Award to an outstanding Maine children's book author or illustrator.

ART, CRAFTS, AND MUSIC

Maine's dramatic coast has always been a favorite subject for artists. One, Winslow Homer (1836–1910), had a studio and home in Prout's Neck. He's best known for his scenes of people struggling against the powerful sea. Artist Andrew Wyeth (1917–) has long kept a summer home in Cushing, painting the landscapes and people he saw in the area.

Handcrafts have a long tradition in Maine. One is the Native American art of basketry. Sweetgrass and the wood of the brown ash tree are the main materials used. Typically, men cut down the trees and pounded the logs until the wood splintered. Women wove the grass and the splints, or strips of wood, into practical items such as potato-carrying baskets and fishing traps. European settlers found the baskets useful and often bought them from the Native people. Today, the Maine Indian Basketmakers Alliance preserves the ancient art of basketry. The group teaches its basketmaking traditions to others, too.

Boatbuilding is another Maine tradition. Native Americans built birch bark canoes that traveled both the rivers and the ocean. In 1607, English colonists at

SEE IT HERE!

THE WYETH CENTER

See three generations of Wyeth paintings at the Wyeth Center at Rockland's Farnsworth Museum. Andrew Wyeth belongs to a family of artists. His father, N. C. Wyeth, was a painter and illustrator of classic books such as *Robinson Crusoe* and *Treasure Island*, and his son Jamie Wyeth is a contemporary realist painter. Many of their paintings feature outdoor Maine scenes, and the Wyeth Center displays their work.

SEE IT HERE!

ARTISTIC TRADITIONS

Want to see authentic basketry, carvings, and beadwork by Wabanaki artists? Then visit the Wabanaki Arts Center Gallery. It's in Old Town on Indian Island. This gallery displays the work of more than 70 Wabanaki artists. Each piece represents the rich culture and traditions of Maine's Native people. Purchases at the gallery benefit the Maine Indian Basketmakers Alliance.

Popham built the *Virginia,* the first ship constructed in Maine. In time, shipbuilding became an important Maine industry. While steel ships have largely replaced wooden vessels, some Mainers still practice the centuries-old tradition of wooden boatbuilding. The WoodenBoat School in Brooklin offers courses in boatbuilding and related woodcrafts. Skilled craftspeople are still building wooden boats in Boothbay Harbor, Portland, Bath, and other communities.

Maine also has a tradition of making musical instruments. A craftsman in Bangor first made a violin around 1800. More violin making led to the formation of a violin makers' association in 1916. Today, Maine craftspeople are still making stringed instruments such as violins, guitars, mandolins, and harps. Lumberjack songs and sea shanties, or rhythmic sailors' songs, are part of Maine's musical history, too. The Maine Folklife Center preserves many old recordings of these traditional tunes.

Craftspeople at the WoodenBoat School in Brooklin

Jonathan Cooper, a violin maker in Gorham, crafts one of his instruments.

The Bangor Symphony Orchestra, founded in 1896, is the oldest community orchestra in the country. Portland also has a symphony orchestra, as well as an opera company and chamber music ensembles. Rockland is proud to be the birthplace of classical music composer Walter Piston. Two of his symphonies won Pulitzer Prizes. Rockland also hosts a blues festival, and Bangor holds an annual jazz festival. Many other classical, blues, folk, ethnic, bluegrass, jazz, and pop music events are held around the state.

SPORTS

Maine's professional sports teams aren't well known around the country, but Mainers are proud of their American Hockey League team, the Portland Pirates. Baseball fans cheer the Portland Sea Dogs, a double-A team affiliated with the Boston Red Sox. Some Mainers have made it to baseball's major leagues. In the 1890s, Louis Sockalexis was a leading pitcher and hitter for the Cleveland Spiders. And Carl "Stump" Merrill managed

MINI-BIO

LOUIS SOCKALEXIS: PENOBSCOT BASEBALL CHAMP

Louis Sockalexis (1871–1913), a Penobscot from Old Town on Indian Island, often had to deal with insults and jeers from the crowd when he stepped onto the field. But ignorant jeers turned to enthusiastic cheers when Sockalexis swatted home runs, pitched three no-hitters, and stole bases. Sockalexis was the first Native American to play on a Major League Baseball team. He played for the Cleveland Spiders from 1897 to 1899.

Want to know more? See http://people.maine.com/publius/almanac/encycweb/htm/soclalex.htm

the New York Yankees (1990–1991) and several of their minor-league affiliates. Another type of sport appeals to Ricky Craven of Newburgh. He's a champion race-car driver.

With its mountains, woods, and waterways, Maine is a great place for outdoor sports. Winter is the time for snowmobiling, skiing, and ice-skating. Many international skiing competitions are held at Sugarloaf Mountain near Carrabassett.

Mainers support local teams such as the Portland Sea Dogs, seen here in action against the Connecticut Defenders.

Skiers glide down the slopes at Sugarloaf.

Ice hockey is a favorite sport, too. Summer brings sport fishing and sailboat, canoe, and kayak racing. In August, Castine hosts the annual Retired Skippers' Race. Jonesport holds the World's Fastest Lobster Boat Races on the Fourth of July. Whether they're taking part in a sport or just watching, Mainers know how to have fun!

READ ABOUT

Penobscot and Passamaquoddy leaders visit the state legislature to discuss mutual respect and equal rights.

CHAPTER SEVEN

GOVERNMENT

★

IN THE 1700S, MAINERS LOOKED FORWARD TO THEIR TOWN MEETINGS. These meetings were the way people carried on local government. Town meetings were great social events, too. Starting in March, after the long, cold winter, they gave people a chance to catch up on community news and renew old friendships. This type of government has been called the "purest form of democracy." Over the years, Maine's state government became more complex. But Maine still carries on much of its local government through town meetings.

FAQ

Q: WHAT'S THE DIFFERENCE BETWEEN A CAPITAL AND A CAPITOL?

A: Capital—spelled with an a—is a city that's the seat of government. Capitol—spelled with an o—is a building that houses important government offices.

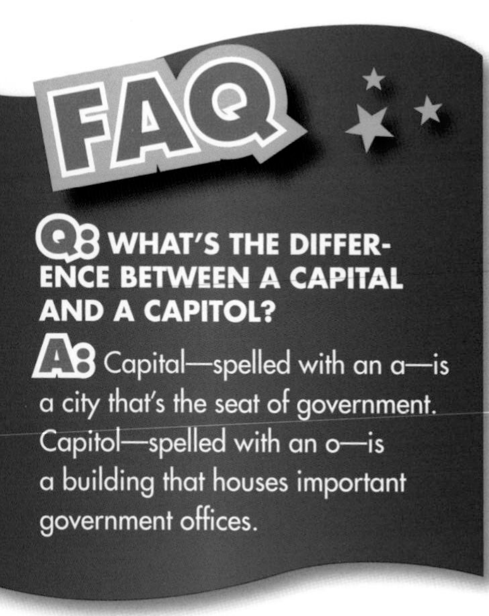

THE CAPITAL AND THE CAPITOL

When Maine first became a state in 1820, Portland became its capital city. That's where the state government offices were located. Portland was chosen because it was Maine's biggest city. State government leaders met in Portland's statehouse. Soon, state lawmakers began to look for a new, more centrally located capital. They chose Augusta in 1827, and it's still Maine's capital city today.

A grand state capitol, with tall columns and a dome on top, was built to house the lawmakers. Mainers call their capitol the State House. The governor's offices are in the State House, too.

Like the U.S. government, Maine's state government is split into three branches—legislative, executive, and judicial. Each branch helps balance the other two. This way, no one branch can gain too much power.

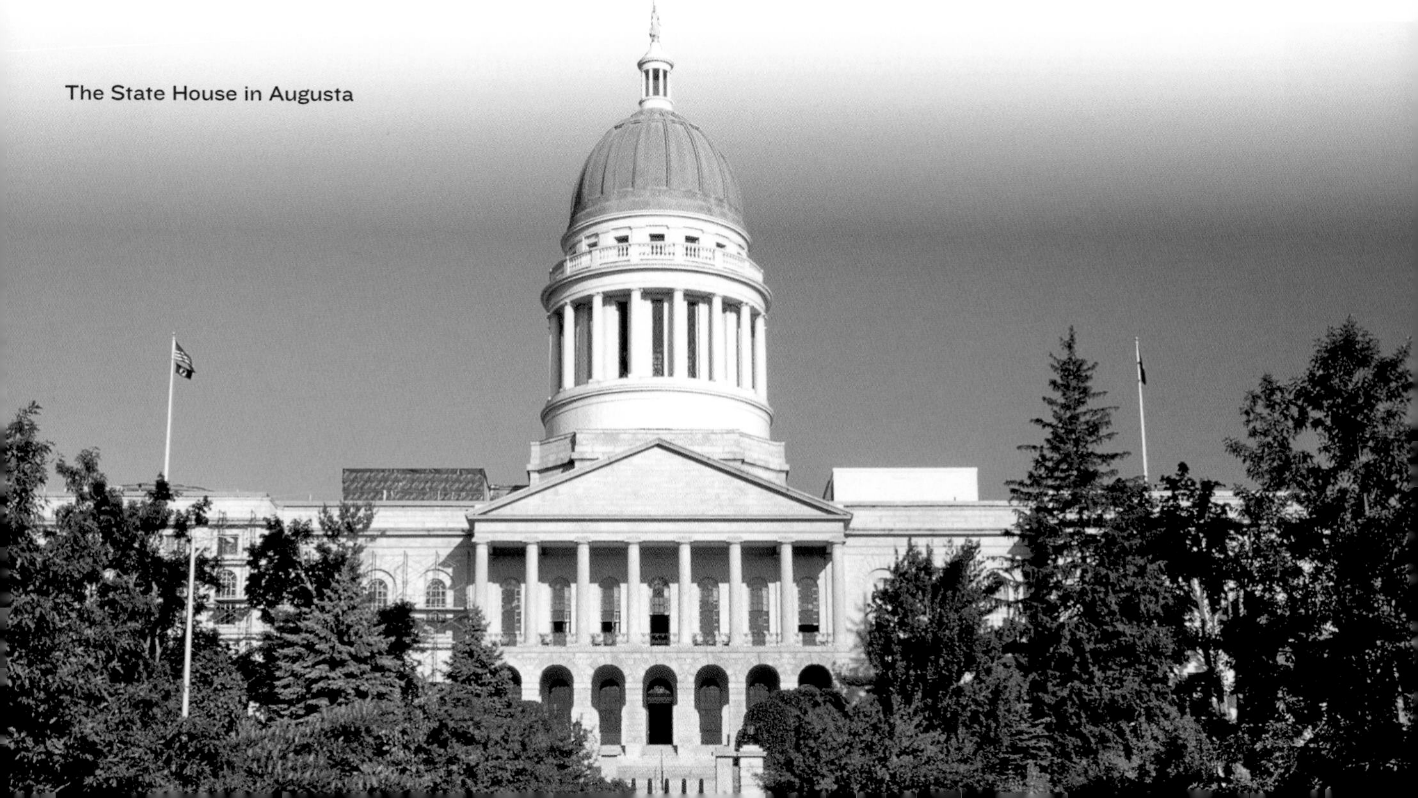

The State House in Augusta

THE LEGISLATIVE BRANCH

The job of the legislative branch is to make state laws. Maine's legislature, like the U.S. Congress, is bicameral. That is, it's made up of two houses—the 35-member senate and the 151-member house of representatives. Both houses meet in the State House in Augusta.

Voters from all over the state elect senators and representatives from their districts. This system makes sure that all citizens are represented in the legislature. All legislators are elected to a two-year term. They may serve up to four terms in a row.

Capitol Facts

Here are some fascinating facts about Maine's state capitol.

Capitol's official name: . . . . State House
Height: . . . . 185 feet (56 m)
Width: . . . . 300 feet (91 m)
Number of stories high: 4
Top structure: . . . . A circular tower capped with a dome
On top of that: . . . . A statue of the female goddess Wisdom
Original architect: . . . . Charles Bulfinch
Original building material: . . . . Hallowell granite
Construction dates: 1828–1832
Cost of construction: $139,000
Major renovation: 1911
Location: . . . . Corner of Capitol and State streets, Augusta

Capital City

This map shows places of interest in Augusta, Maine's capital city.

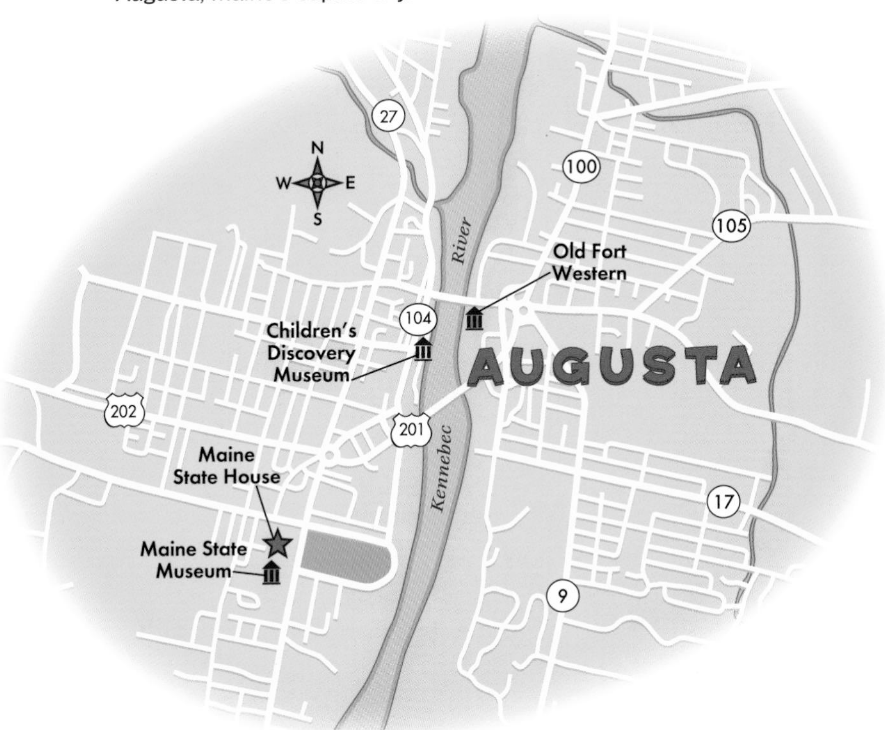

SEE IT HERE!

THE HALL OF FLAGS

Stop by Maine's State House in Augusta. Like many visitors, you may find yourself drawn to the Hall of Flags. This great hall is on the building's second floor. It displays the flags of Maine's military units that served in the Civil War, World War I, World War II, and others. The flags honor the many men and women of Maine who served their country in wartime. Other historic flags can be seen in the Maine State Museum, just south of the State House.

MINI-BIO

MARGARET CHASE SMITH: A LEADER WITH A CONSCIENCE

It was 1950. A woman took to the Senate floor and delivered her "Declaration of Conscience" speech. It condemned Senator Joseph McCarthy's anticommunist campaign. This speech brought Margaret Chase Smith (1897–1995) to national attention. A native of Skowhegan, she represented Maine in the U.S. House of Representatives (1940–1949) and the U.S. Senate (1949–1973). She was the first woman ever elected to the U.S. Senate and the first woman to serve in both houses of Congress.

Want to know more? See www.mcslibrary.org/bio/biolong.htm

THE EXECUTIVE BRANCH

Maine's executive branch makes sure the laws are carried out. It is headed by the governor, who serves a four-year term. Governors can serve only two terms in a row, but there is no limit on the total number of terms they can serve. If the governor dies or leaves office, the president of the state senate becomes governor.

Education leaders and others applaud as Governor John Baldacci signs the state budget in January 2007.

Maine's government has many executive officers, but the governor is the only one who's elected by the voters. The secretary of state, the attorney general, the treasurer, and the auditor are elected by the legislature. The governor appoints most of the other department heads in the executive branch. They oversee areas such as education, taxation, state parks, and the environment.

Representing Maine

This list shows the number of elected officials who represent Maine, both on the state and national levels.

OFFICE	NUMBER	LENGTH OF TERM
State senators	35	2 years
State representatives	151	2 years
U.S. senators	2	6 years
U.S. representatives	2	2 years
Presidential electors	4	—

MINI-BIO

EDMUND MUSKIE: THE BAREFOOT BOY FROM MAINE

He was the son of a Rumford tailor, and he went far. Edmund Muskie (1914–1996) became Maine's governor (1955–1959) and a U.S. senator (1959–1980). A fellow senator liked to call him the "barefoot boy from Maine." Other people called him Mr. Clean because he tried to control pollution. In 1968, Muskie ran for vice president with presidential candidate Hubert Humphrey, but they lost. Muskie went on to become U.S. secretary of state (1980–1981) under President Jimmy Carter.

Want to know more? See www.maine.gov/sos/kids/allabout/people/e_muskie.htm

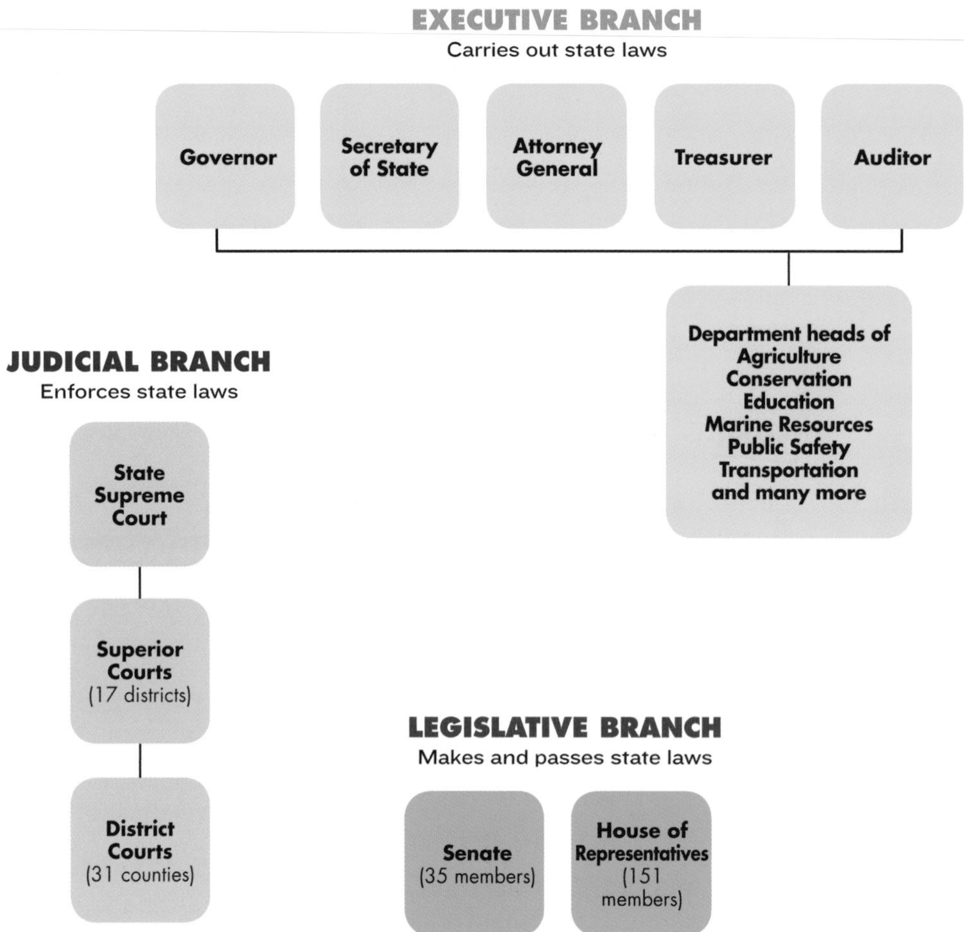

THE JUDICIAL BRANCH

The judicial branch is made up of judges who preside over courts. Their job is to apply the law. When someone is accused of a crime, the judges examine the law and decide whether the person has broken it. In a trial before a jury, the judge makes sure the trial proceeds in a lawful manner.

Maine Counties

This map shows the 16 counties in Maine. Augusta, the state capital, is indicated with a star.

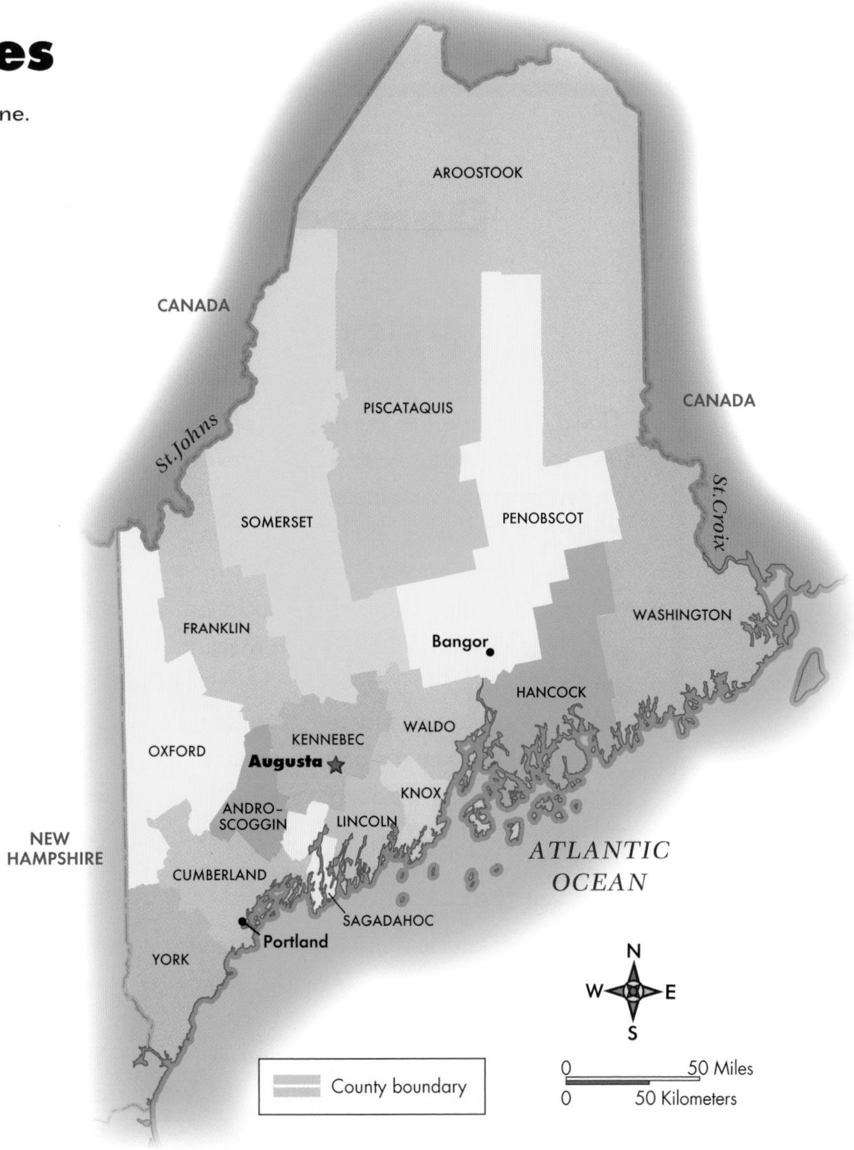

AROOSTOOK
CANADA
PISCATAQUIS
CANADA
St. Johns
St. Croix
SOMERSET
PENOBSCOT
FRANKLIN
WASHINGTON
Bangor
HANCOCK
WALDO
KENNEBEC
OXFORD
Augusta
KNOX
ANDRO-SCOGGIN
LINCOLN
NEW HAMPSHIRE
ATLANTIC OCEAN
CUMBERLAND
SAGADAHOC
Portland
YORK
N W E S
County boundary
0 50 Miles
0 50 Kilometers

The supreme judicial court is Maine's highest court. It has a chief justice, or judge, and six associate justices. People who are not pleased with decisions of lower courts may appeal their cases to the supreme judicial court. Maine's superior courts are the only courts that handle jury trials. They also hear appeals from lower courts. District courts handle minor cases, as well as juvenile offenders and divorce cases. The governor appoints judges to all these courts, with the approval of the state senate.

Maine has more than 400 communities known as unorganized townships. They have no government structure at all, and they elect no local officials. The state supervises their schools, and the county is in charge of their roads.

THINK ABOUT IT!

Town Meetings: Democracy or Disaster?

PRO

"Town Meeting is the 'purest form of democracy,' because citizens, not their representatives, participate directly in the making of their laws and the raising and spending of their taxes."

—Maine Municipal Association, Citizens' Guide to Town Meeting

"We must make sure that our proposals are acceptable to a majority of citizens in our town. . . . If we don't do our homework and craft plans . . . that reflect public opinion, . . . then we won't get our proposals adopted."

—Dan Fleishman, Town Planner, Arundel, Maine

Mainers are proud of their tradition of town meetings. They truly enjoy government by the people. And public officials know they must get the citizens' approval on any project they want to carry out.

CON

"In some towns . . . town meeting participation has dropped markedly. . . . Without broad participation in decisionmaking, there is no guarantee that government can actually carry out the wishes of those it represents."

—Maine Municipal Association, Local Government in Maine

"[Biddeford] was growing so rapidly that new questions were constantly arising for which the selectmen had no power of decision. . . . Biddeford had grown too large to be governed by mass meetings."

—Dane Yorke, *A History and Stories of Biddeford*

Some Mainers believe town meetings don't work. They say that too few people attend. Others point out that larger towns have too many issues for ordinary citizens to deal with.

Erik Anderson (left), a student at Messalonskee High School in Oakland, sings the national anthem before a town meeting in Rome.

LOCAL GOVERNMENT

Maine is divided into 16 counties. Voters in each county elect three county commissioners, a county attorney, a sheriff, and a treasurer.

Maine has 22 communities that are officially called cities. Most cities elect a mayor or city manager and a city council. Each city has home rule. That is, it can draw up its own charter, or basic set of laws, without getting the approval of the legislature.

Maine also has about 430 towns. Most towns are governed by town meetings. In these meetings, citizens come together to elect officials called selectmen, as well as a tax collector, a school board, and other officials. They also hold votes to decide on local issues such as taxes and spending.

Plantations are another unit of local government. They're groups of small, rural communities that are sparsely populated. Residents hold town meetings and elect assessors to handle day-to-day governing tasks. In addition, Maine's Native Americans carry on their own tribal government in units called Indian nations. Few states have as many unusual types of local government as Maine has. But these systems work well for Mainers—just as they have for more than 200 years.

State Flag

Maine's state flag features the state seal against a deep-blue field. This color is the same shade of blue that appears on the U.S. flag. Maine officially adopted this flag design in 1909.

State Seal

Maine's state seal features a shield showing a pine tree with a moose reclining at the foot of the tree. The pine tree stands for the rich forest resources of the Maine woods, and the moose represents the state's abundant wildlife.

To the left of the shield is a farmer. He leans on a scythe, or long-handled blade for cutting grass. To the right is a sailor leaning on an anchor. They represent two traditional ways of life in Maine—farming and seafaring.

Above the shield is the North Star. This is another sign of Maine's seafaring history. Ships at sea could find their way by keeping sight of the bright North Star. The star also represents Maine's northerly location. (When it entered the Union, Maine was the nation's northernmost state.) Beneath the star is a banner with the state motto, *"Dirigo."* That's Latin for "I lead," "I direct," or "I guide." This motto has a double meaning. On the one hand, it refers to the North Star's guiding light. It also refers to the state of Maine as a guiding force for its citizens. Underneath the shield is a banner with the name Maine.

READ ABOUT

This worker in Dresden is harvesting blueberries in areas that are difficult for mechanical harvesters.

ECONOMY

★

HOW WOULD YOU LIKE A NICE, JUICY SLICE OF BLUEBERRY PIE? How about some blueberry pancakes drowning in blueberry syrup? Those are taste treats that Mainers are proud of. Maine is the largest producer of wild blueberries in the nation—and in the whole world! Blueberries are just one of the products that make Maine's economy strong. Other products range from seafood to paper to toothpicks!

A farmer checks his potato crop in Aroostook County.

FARM PRODUCTS

Wild blueberries have been growing in Maine for centuries. Native Americans ate them and introduced them to English settlers. Today, Maine grows 98 percent of the nation's wild, or low-bush, blueberries. Their flavor is much more intense than the **cultivated** blueberries sold in most supermarkets. Most of Maine's blueberries grow in Washington County. The bushes cover vast, rolling plains called blueberry barrens. Every August, Mi'kmaq people join local families to harvest the blueberries by raking the barrens.

Maine is a top potato producer, too. Potatoes are the state's leading crop. Most potato farms are in Aroostook County. Milk and eggs are some other important farm products. Maine's tree farms are busy during the winter holidays. They sell thousands of Christmas trees and wreaths.

Maple syrup is another Maine product. For centuries, Native Americans tapped maple trees, or drew out the sweet sap and made it into syrup. This was yet another skill the Indians taught to white settlers. By 2006, Maine ranked second (after Vermont) in the nation in maple syrup production.

WORDS TO KNOW

cultivated *raised as a crop on a farm*

Aroostook County's potato harvest begins in the fall. Some schools even let students out of school to help with the harvest!

Major Agricultural and Mining Products

This map shows where Maine's major agricultural and mining products come from. See a chicken? That means poultry is raised there.

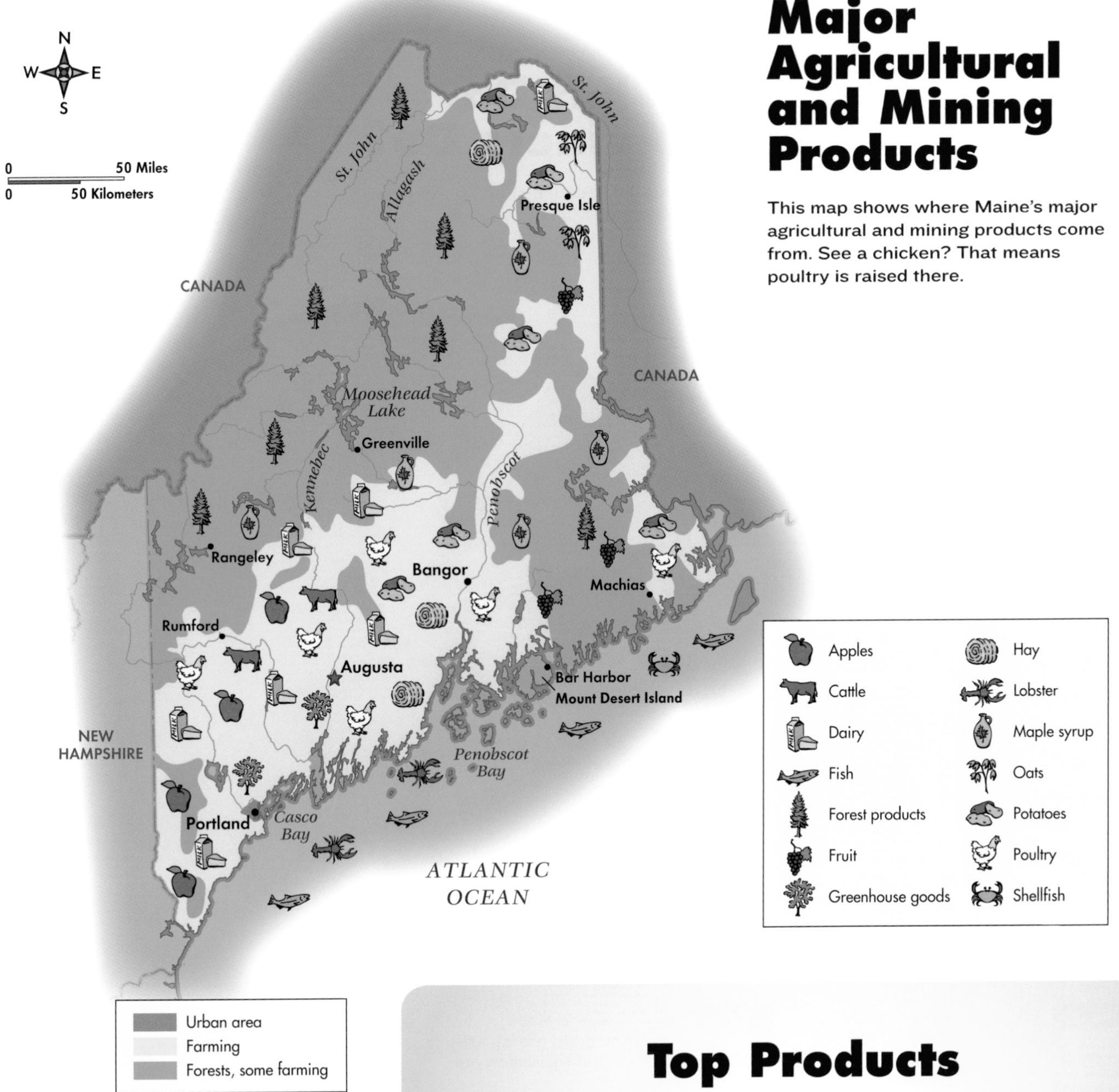

Top Products

Agriculture Milk and other dairy products, potatoes, eggs, greenhouse and nursery products, blueberries

Manufacturing Paper and pulp, food products, ships and boats, computer and electronic equipment

Mining Sand and gravel, cement, crushed stone, granite

Fishing Lobsters, salmon, clams, herring

SEE IT HERE!

THE PORTLAND FISH EXCHANGE

Early in the morning, fishing boats pull up to the pier. Here at the Portland Fish Exchange, millions of pounds of fish are sold every year. The sunburned crew members unload their catch, lifting brightly colored barrels full of fish or shellfish up to the dock. Inside the exchange, workers have been busy since before sunrise. They separate the different species, weigh the catches, and arrange them in the refrigerated warehouse. Then buyers come in and decide what they want to buy. The fish are sold by auction—that is, a batch goes to the highest bidder. Within hours, products are on their way to restaurants, markets, and processing plants.

What Do Mainers Do?

This color-coded chart shows what industries Mainers work in.

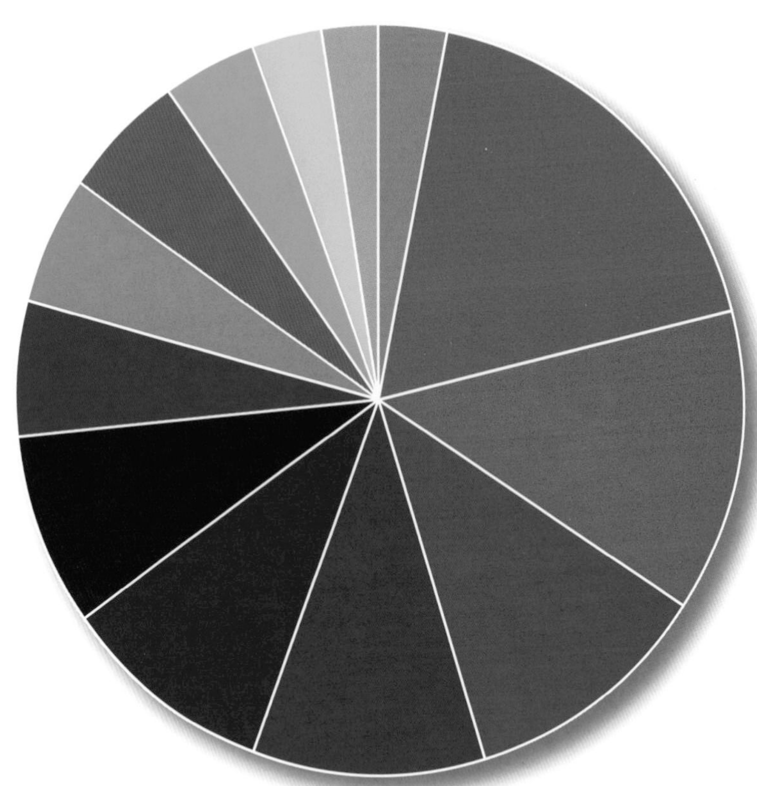

- **25.3%** Educational services, health care, and social assistance, 166,076
- **13.8%** Retail trade, 90,547
- **10.3%** Manufacturing, 67,194
- **8.4%** Construction, 55,224
- **7.9%** Arts, entertainment, recreation, accommodation, and food services, 51,584
- **7.4%** Professional, scientific, management, and administrative and waste management services, 48,303
- **6.4%** Finance, insurance, real estate, rental, and leasing, 41,831
- **4.6%** Other services, except public administration, 29,926
- **4.3%** Public administration, 28,119
- **4.3%** Transportation, warehousing, and utilities, 28,194
- **3.2%** Wholesale trade, 20,773
- **2.3%** Agriculture, forestry, fishing, hunting, and mining, 15,277
- **1.8%** Information, 11,880

Source: U.S. Census Bureau, 2006

Fishers hauling in their catch

FISHING

"It's what I know," says the brawny captain of a fishing boat. "I'm not going to do anything else." That's the feeling of many of Maine's fishers. They brave nasty weather and icy waves, often spending days or weeks at sea to bring in their catches.

As lobsters grow, they shed their shell and grow a bigger one. A lobster sheds its shell eight times in the first year of its life!

You'll see fishing boats in every harbor along the coast. Fishing has been a major industry in Maine for more than two centuries. Lobsters are the state's most valuable catch. In 2005, Maine lobster fishers landed more than 67 million pounds (30 million kilograms) of lobster, valued at more than $300 million!

Salmon, herring, cod, haddock, pollock, and flounder are some of the major fish catches. Shellfish such as clams, mussels, shrimps, and oysters are valuable, too. Much of the fish and shellfish caught in Maine is sold at a massive market called the Portland Fish Exchange.

GOING LOBSTERING

Today, lobster is considered a luxury food. But for Maine's Native Americans, lobster was just a practical material. When they went fishing, they used lobster meat to bait their hooks. On land, they used ground-up lobster to fertilize their crops!

In colonial times, people thought of lobster as "poverty food." The lowly lobster was fed to servants and prisoners. At one point, servants in Massachusetts were so sick of eating lobster that they rose up in protest. They demanded that their work contracts include a special condition: they would not be made to eat lobster more than three times a week!

By the early 1800s, people in New York City and Boston valued lobster as a fine food. That's when Maine's lobster industry really took off. Lobster fishers called smackmen entered the scene. They were named after their boats, called smacks. A smack had a tank with holes drilled in the sides so seawater could come in. Live lobsters were stored there as the smackmen transported them to New York and Boston.

Lobster pounds began to appear along the coast of Maine in the 1870s. These were holding tanks with water flowing through them. Lobsters could be kept there until they were ready to be sold. Dozens of lobster pounds operate in Maine today.

Cooking lobster in Trenton

Logs ready for processing at the Boise Cascade Paper Plant in Rumford

FORESTRY

Where do most of our toothpicks come from? If you guessed Maine, you're right! Maine is the biggest producer of toothpicks in the nation. With forests covering most of the state, Maine has a booming forest-products industry. Large companies and individual farmers own most of Maine's forestland. Some of the major species used for commercial purposes are spruce, fir, maple, birch, aspen, oak, and pine.

MILTON BRADLEY: GAME MAKER

Do you like to play board games? If so, you can thank Milton Bradley (1836–1911) of Vienna, Maine. He started the board game industry when he invented a game called The Checkered Game of Life in 1860. His Milton Bradley Company went on to produce Scrabble, Yahtzee, Battleship, Chutes and Ladders, and other popular games. Bradley also developed games to help with early childhood development. He invented the paper cutter, too.

Want to know more? See www.invent.org/hall_of_fame/252.html

MANUFACTURING INDUSTRY

One day in 1911, Leon Leonwood (L. L.) Bean came back from a hunting trip with cold, wet feet and a big idea. He'd attach leather to the top of his rubber boots to keep the moisture out. He called his new boot the Maine hunting shoe and began mailing out flyers to sell it to hunters. Bean went on to develop and sell many products, including cloth-

Shoppers outside the L. L. Bean store in Freeport

This paper mill in Houlton is one of Maine's many lumber-processing factories.

ing and gear for camping, fishing, and other rugged outdoor activities. He believed in customer satisfaction, and if a customer wasn't happy with a product, Bean provided a refund or a replacement. Soon the L.L. Bean company came to stand for quality and service. Today, outdoor enthusiasts around the world shop at the L.L. Bean store in Freeport, either in person or by mail order.

It's no surprise, though, that forest-based products are Maine's leading factory goods. Maine's forest trees go to factories and mills. There the wood is made into products as diverse as paper, lumber, toothpicks, clothespins, and lobster traps.

Paper and pulp are the top factory products. (Pulp is ground-up wood used to make paper products.) Maine is the number-two producer of paper in the country, after Wisconsin. Maine's paper mills turn out many different types of paper. They may end up as newspapers, magazines, books, cardboard boxes, paper bags, tissue paper, bank checks, or microwave popcorn bags!

MINI-BIO

PERCY SPENCER: MICROWAVE MAN

Imagine a microwave oven that weighs 750 pounds (340 kg) and stands 5 feet 6 inches (1.7 m) high! That's how big the first microwave oven was. Percy Spencer (1894–1970) invented it in 1945. However, it took years before the oven could be made small enough for convenient household use. Spencer was an electronics genius who developed 120 inventions in his lifetime. But he's best known for inventing the microwave oven. Spencer was born in Howland.

Want to know more? See www.invent.org/Hall_Of_Fame/136.html

Tourmaline

Food products are next in importance. Maine's food plants process many of the state's crops and fishing products. Baked beans and chowder are cooked and canned. Blueberries, apples, and potatoes are packed for shipping. Lobsters and fish are frozen, canned, or shipped fresh.

Boat- and shipbuilding are still important industries, just as they have been since the 1700s. Bath Iron Works, a shipbuilder in Bath, is the state's largest private employer. Portsmouth Naval Shipyard is another shipbuilding facility. Both make huge seagoing vessels. Many boatyards along the coast make private boats and yachts. Other Maine factory products include computer chips, aircraft parts, and shoes and other leather goods.

MINING

In 1820, two boys were wandering through the countryside in Paris, Maine. They came upon a tree that had fallen over, with its roots covered with soil. Something green was glistening in that soil. It turned out to be specks of a valuable gemstone called tourmaline! The Mount Mica tourmaline mine was founded on that site in 1822. It was the nation's first gemstone mine.

In 2004, Maine ranked 12th in the nation in gemstone production. Tourmaline is still the state's most valuable gem, and it's also the official state

Workers blasting granite in a quarry near Stonington

gem. It comes in a wide range of colors, from black and white to pink and violet to blue and green. The Mount Mica mine is still going strong, and a mine near Newry has one of the largest deposits of tourmaline in the world.

Maine's leading mining products—sand and gravel—may not be as exciting as gems, but they're more valuable. They're used to build roads and to make building materials such as bricks and concrete pipes. Sand and gravel come in handy during Maine's chilly winters, too. They are spread on snowy, icy roads to make them safe for drivers. Some of the raw materials for Portland cement (a type of cement used in concrete and mortar) and crushed stone are mined in Maine.

Mainers mine a few other materials on a small scale. They include slate, a gray rock used on roofs and patios, and granite, a hard stone used for monuments and buildings. Maine was once the nation's top granite producer, and buildings all over the country have been built with granite from Maine. That includes libraries, post offices, churches, and museums. They stand as monuments to the industry and dedication of hardworking Mainers.

Interstate highway
95
N
W
E
S
0
50 Miles
0
50 Kilometers
St. Lawrence
CANADA
CANADA
NEW HAMPSHIRE
ATLANTIC OCEAN
St. John
St. John
Allagash
Moosehead Lake
Kennebec
Penobscot
St. Croix
Androscoggin
Madawaska
Fort Kent
Van Buren
Allagash
Caribou
Presque Isle
Ashland
Mars Hill
Houlton
Millinocket
Jackman
Greenville
The Forks
Geographic Center of Maine
Calais
Rangeley
Kingfield
Orono
Eastport
Skowhegan
Madison
Bangor
Machias
Farmington
Norridgewock
Rumford
Ellsworth
Bethel
Waterville
Castine
Livermore
Belfast
Bar Harbor
Augusta
Mount Desert Island
Monmouth
Rockland
Fryeburg
Lewiston
Thomaston
Naples
Auburn
Damariscotta
Isle Au Haut
Brunswick
Cushing
Freeport
Vinalhaven Island
Yarmouth
Bath
Boothbay Harbor
Westbrook
Portland
South Portland
Cape Elizabeth
Saco
Scarborough
Sanford
Biddeford
Old Orchard Beach
Kennebunkport
South Berwick
Kennebunk
Kittery

TRAVEL GUIDE

★

ROCKY, WAVE-SWEPT CLIFFS AND QUIET FISHING VILLAGES, DEEP FORESTS AND SPARKLING LAKES—THESE ARE SOME OF THE REASONS PEOPLE LOVE TO VISIT MAINE. It's the perfect place to search for a moose, climb up to the top of a lighthouse, enjoy a lobster festival, or visit a Native American museum. Here's a travel guide to help you explore the state of Maine—whether you're on the road or curled up in a comfy chair!

← Follow along with this travel map. We'll begin in Madawaska and travel all the way around the state to Eastport!

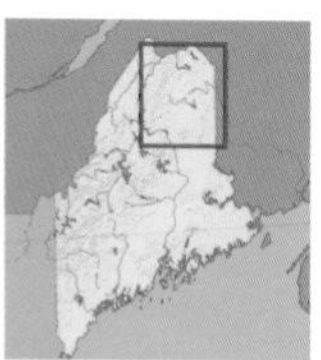

AROOSTOOK COUNTY

THINGS TO DO: Zoom along snowmobile trails, canoe through a haunting wilderness, wander around an Acadian village, or see how loggers used to work.

Madawaska

★ **Tante Blanche Museum:** At this museum, you'll learn all about the history and heritage of Madawaska's French Acadian settlers. They arrived from Nova Scotia in 1785, and most of the people in town are their descendants.

★ **Acadian Festival:** Come in late June and celebrate Acadian culture in Maine's most French town. Enjoy Acadian music, costumed dancers, and food!

Allagash

★ **Allagash Wilderness Waterway:** Whether you like whitewater rafting or leisurely canoeing, you'll enjoy mile after mile of lush wilderness here along the Allagash River.

Canoeing on the Allagash Wilderness Waterway

Caribou

★ **Nylander Museum:** This museum is devoted to Maine's natural history. Displays feature minerals, fossils, seashells, and mammals and birds from the region. In the summer, the museum offers free guided nature walks.

★ **Lakes and Snowmobile Trails:** Caribou is the entryway to the northern lakes region. The town is jam-packed with snowmobile clubs! In the winter, you can follow the region's snowmobile trails for miles. More than 1,600 miles (2,575 km) of well-groomed trails wind through the woods of Aroostook County.

Fort Kent

★ **Fort Kent Blockhouse:** This national historic landmark was built in 1839, when Maine almost went to war with Canada.

Van Buren

★ **Acadian Historic Village:** This village highlights the area's French Acadian heritage. Wander through its 16 reconstructed buildings, and you'll see how Maine's Acadians used to live.

Presque Isle

★ **Northern Maine Museum of Science:** This museum on the University of Maine campus houses a model of the sun. It's the starting point for the Maine Solar System Model, which extends for 40 miles (64 km) across Aroostook County!

SEE IT HERE!

THE MAINE SOLAR SYSTEM MODEL

Drive along Highway 1, and you'll pass one model planet after another. They belong to the world's largest complete three-dimensional scale model of the solar system. Each planet is the proper distance from the sun, according to a scale of 93 million to 1! Perched on poles, the planets and other solar system objects may be in potato fields, parking lots, or car dealerships. Sizes are perfectly to scale, too. The sun, in Presque Isle's Northern Maine Museum of Science, measures 49.5 feet (15 m) across. Earth, to the south, is the size of a grapefruit. The dwarf planet Pluto, in Houlton, is the size of a walnut, and its little moon Charon is the size of a pea.

Ashland

★ **Ashland Logging Museum:** Here you'll learn about northern Maine's logging and lumbering history and see tools and equipment the loggers used.

Houlton

★ **Market Square District:** Here you'll see many historic buildings from the old logging days. Many ornate mansions in Houlton have been preserved, too. Back in the early 1900s, Houlton was one of the 10 richest communities in the nation!

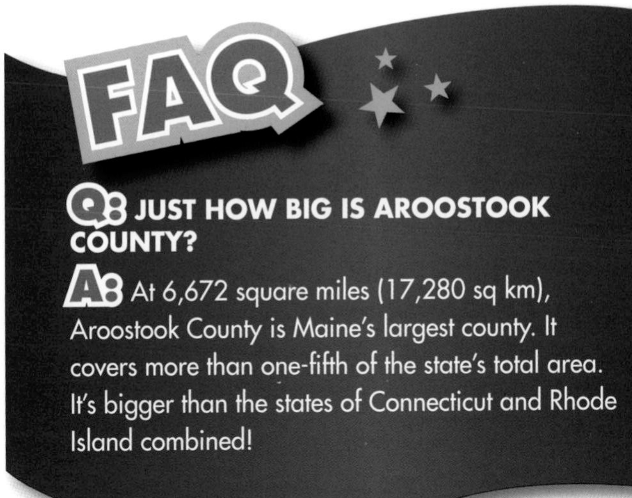

FAQ

Q8 JUST HOW BIG IS AROOSTOOK COUNTY?

A8 At 6,672 square miles (17,280 sq km), Aroostook County is Maine's largest county. It covers more than one-fifth of the state's total area. It's bigger than the states of Connecticut and Rhode Island combined!

MOOSEHEAD AND KATAHDIN

THINGS TO DO: Climb Maine's highest peak, hike through snowy woods, spot a moose in the wild, or play Pin the Antlers on the Moose!

Moosehead

★ **Moosehead Lake:** It's the largest freshwater lake in the state and one of Maine's most popular vacation areas. You'll enjoy canoeing and fishing on the lake and hiking through the surrounding forest. If you move quietly, you're sure to see deer and other wildlife. In the winter, people travel the snowy woods on snowmobiles, snowshoes, and even dogsleds!

Greenville

★ **Moose Safari:** Take this guided moose-watching tour from Evergreen Lodge, and you're sure to spot one of these amazing animals. Or just take off moose-watching on your own. May and June are the best times to see them. In this region, moose outnumber humans, three to one!

★ **MooseMainea:** This annual moose festival lasts from mid-May through mid-June. It includes canoe races, the MooseCapades Parade, a Pin the Antlers on the Moose contest, and a mountain bike race called the Tour de Moose!

★ **Steamship *Katahdin*:** Hop aboard the *Katahdin* for a cruise around Moosehead Lake. Or just tour the ship, which is home to the Moosehead Marine Museum.

★ **Moosehead Lake Snofest:** This nine-day winter festival every February features a snowmobile parade, sled dog races, a chowder cook-off, and a chocolate festival.

Millinocket

★ **Baxter State Park:** You can enter the park from either Millinocket or Patten. What's the attraction? It's Mount Katahdin, Maine's highest point. You can see this majestic peak from miles away. About 200 miles (300 km) of hiking trails wind through the park. If you're up for a challenge, hike all the way to the top of the mountain. Your reward is a spectacular view of Maine's natural beauty. Be careful when you walk along the Knife's Edge. It's a narrow footpath atop the mountain!

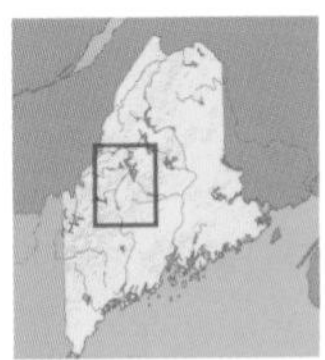

KENNEBEC VALLEY

THINGS TO DO: Ride the river rapids in a raft, swim beneath a crashing waterfall, or tour the State House and its Hall of Flags.

Jackman

★ **Moose River Bow Trip:** From Jackman, you can set out on this several-day wilderness trip by canoe or kayak. Paddlers drift through the unspoiled backwoods, passing moose and coyotes on the way. In the winter, of course, the snowmobiles come out. Jackman is a popular access point for hundreds of miles of groomed snowmobile trails.

The Forks

★ **Rafting outfitters:** This little town on the Kennebec River has more than a dozen rafting companies. They outfit rafters with all they need to take on the area's rushing rivers. This region is Maine's prime spot for whitewater rafting.

★ **Moxie Falls:** It's one of the highest waterfalls in the state, dropping down more than 90 feet (27 m). Take a dip in the swimming hole at the bottom of the falls. The waterfall makes quite a splash there!

Farmington

★ **Earmuffs Parade:** Bring your earmuffs and join the parade on the first Saturday in December! A local resident, Chester Greenwood, invented these useful ear warmers.

Waterville

★ **The Two Cent Bridge:** Be sure to take a walk on this famous, free-swinging footbridge. It crosses the Kennebec between Waterville and Winslow. Workers from Waterville used to take the bridge to their jobs at a Winslow paper mill. They had to pay a toll, though—a whopping two cents!

Two Cent Bridge

Augusta

★ **State House:** Tour this ornate building to see where Maine's lawmakers meet, and wander through the Hall of Flags.

★ **Fort Western:** Built in 1754, this is the oldest wooden fort in New England.

★ **Maine State Museum:** Here you'll explore 12,000 years of history through lifelike exhibits.

WESTERN MOUNTAINS AND LAKES

THINGS TO DO: Learn how maple sugar is made, see waterfalls tumble and splash, catch a trout from your canoe, or watch people throw skillets and chase pigs!

Rangeley

★ **Rangeley Lake State Park:** Fish for trout and salmon in the summer, or go snowshoeing, skiing, or snowmobiling in the winter.

Naples

★ **Sebago Lake State Park:** Fishing, boating, canoeing, swimming, camping, or picnicking—you name it. You'll enjoy it all in this popular natural area.

Bethel

★ **White Mountain National Forest:** Along the hiking trails in this forest, you'll want to stop to admire waterfalls cascading down the mountainsides.

Hiking in the White Mountains

Fryeburg

★ **Fryeburg Fair:** Come in October for Maine's biggest agricultural fair. You'll enjoy rides, games, and entertainment you won't find anywhere else. Watch the horse and pony show, cheer contestants in the skillet throw, or see kids chase little oinkers in the pig scramble!

Livermore

★ **Norlands Living History Museum:** Here you'll get a taste of life in the 1800s. Its buildings include a mansion, a farmer's cottage, a barn, and a one-room schoolhouse. With the help of costumed guides, you'll learn how maple sugar is made, enjoy a harvesttime supper, or watch farmers with their ox-drawn plows.

Lewiston

★ **Bates College:** Bates Coram Library holds the official papers of Maine politician Edmund Muskie. The campus also has an art museum and a concert hall.

SEE IT HERE!

THE FRANCO-AMERICAN HERITAGE CENTER

French culture is alive and well at the Franco-American Heritage Center in Lewiston. The center preserves French Canadian heritage through its museum and year-round cultural programs. One sponsored event is the summertime Festival Franco-Fun. It celebrates French music, culture, and language. The center is housed in the elegant St. Mary's Church, where Lewiston's Catholic French Canadians once worshipped.

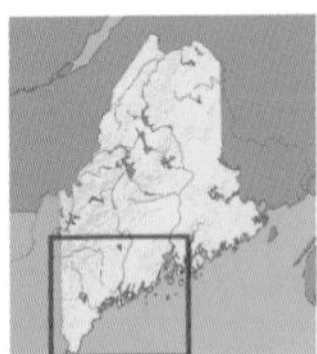

THE SOUTHERN COAST

THINGS TO DO: Lounge on sandy beaches, explore sea life along the rocky coastlines, stroll through charming fishing villages, go on a shopping spree, or paddle a kayak out into the sea.

Kittery

★ **Cobblestone streets:** These old streets remind you that Kittery is one of Maine's oldest cities. First settled in 1623, it's been a shipbuilding center for almost 200 years. Along the streets, you'll find many historic homes.

York

★ **Colonial buildings:** Founded in 1642, York is another historic town. Eight of its colonial buildings—including the old jail, tavern, and warehouse—are now museums.

★ **Cape Neddick Light:** This famous lighthouse is on a little rocky island just beyond York's Cape Neddick. That rocky island is called a nubble, so the lighthouse is nicknamed Nubble Light.

Old Orchard Beach

Old Orchard Beach

★ **The beach:** This is a favorite summer vacation spot, with miles of sandy beaches, as well as shops, rides, and game arcades.

South Portland

★ **Maine Mall:** Shop till you drop at the state's largest mall!

Scarborough

★ **Len Libby Candies:** You'll have a chocolate attack when you see the world's only life-sized chocolate moose!

Cape Elizabeth

★ **Portland Head Light:** This famous lighthouse is one of Maine's most distinctive landmarks. Built in 1791, it's also the state's oldest lighthouse.

Yarmouth

★ **DeLorme Headquarters:** Drop by and see Eartha, the world's largest revolving and rotating globe, measuring more than 41 feet (12.5 m) in diameter!

Portland

★ **Wadsworth-Longfellow House:** Tour the childhood home of the famous poet Henry Wadsworth Longfellow. You'll stroll through the same rooms he did in the 1800s as you go from parlor to drawing room to kitchen and beyond.

★ **Waterfront:** As you stroll along, you'll see the Old Port Exchange and many other historic buildings.

Shopping in Portland's Waterfront District

Freeport

★ **L.L. Bean:** Need a jacket for subzero weather? Need a grill or lantern for camping? Need some snowshoes, a turkey caller, or a kayak? Then head to this world-famous sporting goods store.

★ **Desert of Maine:** You heard it right—it's an actual sandy desert, right here in Maine! Glaciers left the sand behind when they slid through 11,000 years ago. Take a tour around the site, then check out the Sand Museum. It features sand samples from all over the world!

Desert of Maine

Bath

★ **Maine Maritime Museum:** Explore Maine's seafaring history through interactive exhibits and then take a boat cruise.

Boothbay Harbor

★ **Lobster boats, sea kayaks, and cruises:** Lobster boats come and go at this little fishing village. Here you might like to rent a sea kayak to explore the coastline or take a puffin- or whale-watching cruise.

Rockland

★ **Shore Village Museum:** This lighthouse museum displays foghorns, flashing lights, rescue gear, and other lighthouse equipment.

★ **Ferry rides:** Hop aboard a ferry for a ride out to one of the many islands offshore.

CELEBRATE THE LOBSTER!

Do you like lobster? Then head to Rockland during the first weekend in August for the Maine Lobster Festival. Hungry visitors consume more than 25,000 pounds (11,000 kg) of lobster at this popular festival. They also enjoy parades, amusement rides, harbor cruises, a lobster crate race, and much more.

SEE IT HERE!

SEA CREATURES: UP CLOSE AND PERSONAL

Would you like to pet a live shark? Or run your finger across the spiny skin of a sea urchin? Then check out the touch tank at the Maine State Aquarium. This facility is located on the waterfront in West Boothbay Harbor. Its main gallery is built to look like Maine's rocky coast. There you'll see lobsters in all colors and sizes, as well as creatures such as shrimps, red sea anemones, and purple sunstars. For many visitors, the 20-foot (6 m) touch tank is a favorite attraction. After all, how often do you get squirted by a sea cucumber? When this creature is picked up, it's likely to shoot water out of its body!

Anemone

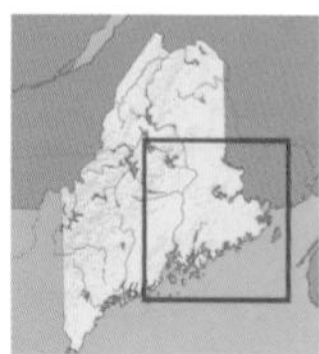

ACADIA AND THE DOWN EAST REGION

THINGS TO DO: See sea captains' homes, visit Revolutionary War sites, see puffins and baby lobsters, or get a glimpse of life in a sawmill town.

Bangor

★ **Maine Forest and Logging Museum:** This museum is built like an old logging and milling community. Here you'll see what life was like in the 1830s, when Bangor was known as the Lumber Capital of the World. Back then, the city had more than 300 sawmills!

★ **Paul Bunyan Statue:** Gaze up at this gigantic statue of the legendary woodsman. He's taller than a three-story building!

Castine

★ **Historical markers:** You'll find more than 100 historical markers in this little town that's steeped in history. The markers pinpoint Revolutionary War battles and other historic events.

★ **Maine Maritime Academy:** Climb aboard its huge training ship, the *State of Maine*, for a tour.

Mount Desert Island

★ **Acadia National Park:** This is a great place for hiking, biking, and wildlife watching. Hike up its forested peaks, and you'll get a breathtaking view of the ocean and coastlands.

★ **Bar Harbor:** Wealthy people used to vacation here, and you can see their mansions along Millionaires' Row.

★ **Mount Desert Oceanarium and Lobster Hatchery:** Watch mother and baby lobsters here to learn more about lobsters' lives. The oceanarium has locations at both Bar Harbor and Southwest Harbor.

Machias

★ **Machias Seal Island:** This island is home to odd little birds called puffins. These colorful, playful seabirds are often called the penguins of New England.

Puffins

★ **Fort O'Brien:** This is the site of the first naval battle of the Revolutionary War.

★ **Burnham Tavern:** This is where colonists planned their attack on the British ship *Margaretta* during the Revolutionary War.

Eastport

★ **Historic districts:** Eastport's two historic districts have dozens of buildings dating from the 1700s and 1800s. Some are the restored homes of sea captains, complete with widow's walks.

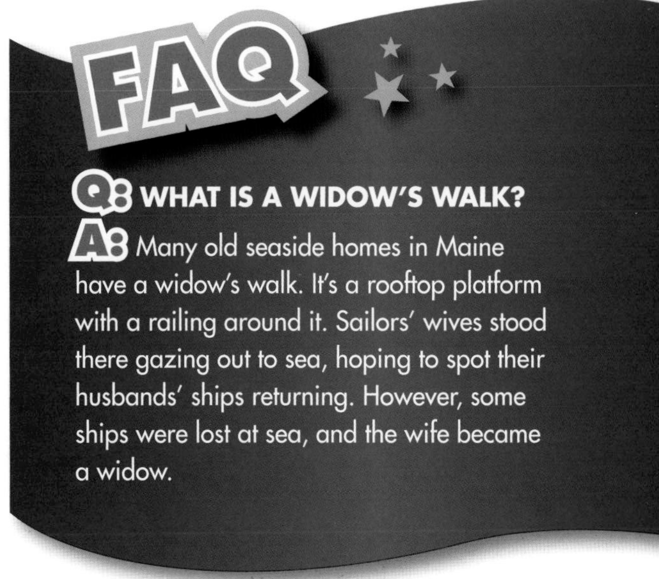

FAQ

Q: WHAT IS A WIDOW'S WALK?

A: Many old seaside homes in Maine have a widow's walk. It's a rooftop platform with a railing around it. Sailors' wives stood there gazing out to sea, hoping to spot their husbands' ships returning. However, some ships were lost at sea, and the wife became a widow.

WRITING PROJECTS

Check out these ideas for creating election brochures and acting out interviews with famous people from the state. Or research explorers and their journeys.

118

ART PROJECTS

119

Learn about the state quarter and design your own, illustrate the state song, or create a great PowerPoint presentation.

TIMELINE

What happened when? This timeline highlights important events in the state's history—and shows what was happening throughout the United States at the same time.

122

GLOSSARY

Remember the Words to Know from the chapters in this book? They're all collected here.

125

FAST FACTS

Use this section to find fascinating facts about state symbols, land area and population statistics, weather, sports teams, and much more.

126

WRITING PROJECTS

★ ★ ★

Create an interview script with a famous person from Maine!

- ★ Research various famous Mainers, such as Stephen King, Patrick Dempsey, Dorothea Dix, Barry Dana, Samantha Smith, Gerald Talbot, and many others.
- ★ Based on your research, pick one person you would most like to interview.
- ★ Write a script of the interview. What questions would you ask? How would this famous person answer? Create a question-and-answer format. You may want to supplement this writing project with a voice recording dramatization of the interview.

SEE: Pages 59, 61, 73 or the Biographical Dictionary on pages133–136.

GO TO: The Maine Historical Society Web site at www.mainehistory.org to find out more about famous public figures from Maine.

Stephen King

Compare and Contrast— When, Why, and How Did They Come?

Compare the migration and explorations of Maine's first people, followed by European explorers and later settlers in Maine. Research:

- ★ When their migrations began
- ★ How they traveled
- ★ Why they migrated
- ★ Where their journeys began and ended
- ★ What they found when they arrived

SEE: Chapters Two and Three, pages 25–35, 37–42.

Create an Election Brochure or Web Site!

Run for office!

Throughout this book you've read about some of the issues that concern Maine today. As a candidate for governor of Maine, create a campaign brochure or Web site.

- ★ Explain how you meet the qualifications to be governor of Maine, and talk about the three or four major issues you'll focus on if you're elected.
- ★ Remember, you'll be responsible for Maine's budget. How would you spend the taxpayers' money?

SEE: Chapter Seven, pages 84–86.

GO TO: Maine's Government Web site at www.maine.gov.

ART PROJECTS

★ ★ ★

Create a PowerPoint Presentation or Visitors' Guide

Welcome to Maine!

Maine is a great place to visit and to live! From its natural beauty to its bustling cities and historic sites, there's plenty to see and do. In your PowerPoint presentation or brochure, highlight 10 to 15 of Maine's stunning landmarks. Be sure to include:

- ★ a map of the state showing where these sites are located
- ★ photos, illustrations, Web links, natural history facts, geographic stats, climate and weather info, and descriptions of plants and wildlife

SEE: Chapters One and Nine, pages 8–21 and 105–115.

GO TO: The official Web site of Maine tourism at www.visitmaine.com. Download and print maps, photos, national landmark images, and vacation ideas for tourists.

Illustrate the Lyrics to the Maine State Song

("State of Maine Song")

Use markers, paints, photos, collage, colored pencils, or computer graphics to illustrate the lyrics to "State of Maine Song," the state song! Turn your illustrations into a picture book, or scan them into a PowerPoint and add music!

SEE: The lyrics to "State of Maine Song" on page 128.

GO TO: The Maine state Web site at www.maine.gov to find out more about the origin of Maine's state song.

Research Maine's State Quarter

From 1999 to 2008, the U.S. Mint introduced new quarters commemorating each of the 50 states in the order they were admitted into the Union. Each state's quarter features a unique design on its reverse, or back.

GO TO: www.usmint.gov/kids and find out what's featured on the back of the Maine quarter.

Research and write an essay explaining:

- ★ the significance of each image
- ★ who designed the quarter
- ★ who chose the final design

Design your own Maine state quarter. What images would you choose for the reverse?

- ★ Make a poster showing the Maine quarter and label each image.

SCIENCE, TECHNOLOGY, & MATH PROJECTS

★ ★ ★

Graph Population Statistics!

★ Compare population statistics (such as ethnic background, birth, death, and literacy rates) in Maine's counties or major cities.

★ In your graph or chart, look at population density, and write sentences describing what the population statistics show; graph one set of population statistics, and write a paragraph explaining what the graphs reveal.

SEE: Chapter Six, pages 66–69.

GO TO: The official Web site for the U.S. Census Bureau at www.census.gov, and at http://quickfacts.census.gov/qfd/states/23000.html, to find out more about population statistics, how they work, and what the statistics are for Maine.

Track Endangered Species

Using your knowledge of Maine's wildlife, research what animals and plants are endangered or threatened. Find out what the state is doing to protect these species. Chart known populations of the animals and plants, and report on changes in certain geographical areas.

SEE: Chapter One, page 22.

GO TO: The Maine Department of Inland Fisheries and Wildlife site at www.maine.gov/ifw/wildlife/species/endangered_species/index.htm or other Maine-specific sites.

Create a Weather Map of Maine!

Use your knowledge of Maine's geography to research and identify conditions that result in specific weather events. Create a weather map or poster that shows the weather patterns over the state. Include a caption explaining the technology used to measure weather phenomena.

SEE: Chapter One, pages 16–17.

GO TO: The National Oceanic and Atmospheric Administration's National Weather Service Web site at www.weather.gov for weather maps and forecasts for Maine.

Portland Head Light in fog

PRIMARY VS. SECONDARY SOURCES

★ ★ ★

What's the Diff?

Your teacher may require at least one or two primary sources and one or two secondary sources for your assignment. So, what's the difference between the two?

- **Primary sources are original.** You are reading the actual words of someone's diary, journal, letter, autobiography, or interview. Primary sources can also be photographs, maps, prints, cartoons, news/film footage, posters, first-person newspaper articles, drawings, musical scores, and recordings. By the way, when you conduct a survey, interview someone, shoot a video, or take photographs to include in a project, you are creating primary sources!
- **Secondary sources are what you find in encyclopedias, textbooks, articles, biographies, and almanacs.** These are written by a person or group of people who tell about something that happened to someone else. Secondary sources also recount what another person said or did. This book is an example of a secondary source.

Now that you know what primary sources are—where can you find them?

- **Your school or local library:** Check the library catalog for collections of original writings, government documents, musical scores, and so on. Some of this material may be stored on microfilm. The Library of Congress Web site (www.loc.gov) is an excellent online resource for primary source materials.
- **Historical societies:** These organizations keep historical documents, photographs, and other materials. Staff members can help you find what you are looking for. History museums are also great places to see primary sources firsthand.
- **The Internet:** There are lots of sites that have primary sources you can download and use in a project or assignment.

TIMELINE

★ ★ ★

U.S. Events

1492
Christopher Columbus and his crew sight land in the Caribbean Sea.

1565
Spanish admiral Pedro Menéndez de Avilés founds St. Augustine, Florida, the oldest continuously occupied European settlement in the continental United States.

1619
The first African indentured laborers in English North America are purchased for work in the Jamestown settlement.

King Philip's War

1400

1500

1600

Maine Events

1400
By this time, several Wabanaki groups live in the region.

1524
Giovanni da Verrazzano reaches the Maine coast.

1604
Frenchmen Samuel de Champlain and Pierre du Guast, Sieur de Monts, establish Maine's first colony on St. Croix Island.

1622
Sir Ferdinando Gorges and Captain John Mason are granted rights to lands that are now Maine and New Hampshire.

1623
The nation's first sawmill is established near York.

1642
Gorges establishes Gorgeana (now York), the first incorporated city in what is now the United States.

1652
Massachusetts annexes the frontier territory that is now Maine.

1675–1676
King Philip's War is fought.

U.S. Events

1682
René-Robert Cavelier, Sieur de La Salle, claims more than 1 million square miles (2.6 million sq km) of territory in the Mississippi River basin for France, naming it Louisiana.

1776
Thirteen American colonies declare their independence from Great Britain.

1846–48
The United States fights a war with Mexico over western territories in the Mexican War.

1886
Apache leader Geronimo surrenders to the U.S. Army, ending the last major Native American rebellion against the expansion of the United States into the West.

1929
The stock market crashes, plunging the United States more deeply into the Great Depression.

1941–45
The United States engages in World War II.

1951–53
The United States engages in the Korean War.

Maine Events

1677
Maine officially becomes a part of Massachusetts.

1700

1775
The first naval battle of the Revolutionary War takes place off the coast of Machias. Benedict Arnold marches through Maine hoping to capture British strongholds in Quebec.

1800

1820
Maine becomes the 23rd U.S. state on March 15.

1842
In the Webster-Ashburton Treaty, the border dispute between Maine and Canada is settled and a new boundary line is drawn.

1866
A fire destroys the Old Port area of downtown Portland.

1888
Maine native Melville W. Fuller becomes the chief justice of the U.S. Supreme Court.

1900

1931
Governor Percival Baxter begins buying land in northern Maine, eventually purchasing more than 90,000 acres (36,000 ha). This land was donated to create Baxter State Park.

1948
Maine's Margaret Chase Smith becomes the first woman elected to the U.S. Senate.

U.S. Events

1964–73
The United States engages in the Vietnam War.

Edmund Muskie

1991
The United States and other nations engage in the brief Persian Gulf War against Iraq.

2000

2001
Terrorists hijack four U.S. aircraft and crash them into the World Trade Center in New York City, the Pentagon in Arlington, Virginia, and a Pennsylvania field, killing thousands.

2003
The United States and coalition forces invade Iraq.

Maine Events

1956
The first U.S. atomic submarine is launched at Kittery-Portsmouth Naval Shipyard.

1964
In supporting Lyndon B. Johnson, Maine favors a Democratic presidential candidate for the first time since 1912.

1974
James Longley becomes the first popularly elected independent governor in U.S. history.

1980
Maine's Edmund Muskie becomes U.S. secretary of state under President Jimmy Carter. In the Indian Land Claims agreement, the U.S. government agrees to pay $81.5 million to Maine's Passamaquoddys, Penobscots, and Maliseets for seized lands.

1984
Joan Benoit Samuelson of Freeport wins the gold medal in the first women's marathon event at the Summer Olympic Games in Los Angeles, California.

1988
Senator George Mitchell of Waterville is named the U.S. Senate majority leader.

2000
Maine passes a bill to lower the costs of prescription drugs.

2003
Maine passes a bill to bring low-cost health insurance to residents by 2009.

GLOSSARY

abolitionist a person who worked to end slavery

breechcloth a garment worn by men over their lower body

cargo trade goods carried on a ship or other vehicle

clipper ships fast sailing ships with tall masts

cultivated raised as a crop on a farm

endangered in danger of becoming extinct

foghorns horns that blast a loud, honking sound as a signal to boaters

glaciers slow-moving masses of ice

hydroelectric power electricity generated by the force of water passing through a dam

medicinal herbs wild plants used to cure various ailments

metamorphic describing rocks that have been changed by extreme pressure, wind, and water

metropolitan area a dense population region that usually includes several towns

negotiate to discuss an issue in order to come to an agreement

peninsula a body of land surrounded by water on three sides but connected to a larger piece of land

precipitation all water that falls to the earth, including rain, sleet, hail, snow, dew, fog, or mist

resin clear or light-colored material that is secreted by trees and other plants; used in varnishes, printing inks, and other products

resource a supply of natural material that helps people live or brings them wealth

spawn to lay eggs

staples essential foods and other supplies

threatened likely to become endangered in the foreseeable future

truce an agreement to hold off from fighting

FAST FACTS

State Symbols

Statehood date	March 15, 1820 the 23rd state
Origin of state name	Descriptive, referring to the mainland as distinct from the many coastal islands
State capital	Augusta
State nickname	Pine Tree State
State motto	*Dirigo* ("I lead")
State animal	Moose
State bird	Black-capped chickadee
State flower	White pinecone and tassel
State fish	Landlocked salmon
State gemstone	Tourmaline
State insect	Honeybee
State song	"State of Maine Song" (see lyrics on page 128)
State tree	White pine

State seal

Geography

Total area; rank	35,385 square miles (91,647 sq km); 39th
Land; rank	30,862 square miles (79,932 sq km); 39th
Water; rank	4,523 square miles (11,715 sq km); 12th
Inland water; rank	2,264 square miles (5,864 sq km); 9th
Coastal water; rank	613 square miles (1,588 sq km); 9th
Territorial water; rank	1,647 square miles (4,266 sq km); 6th
Geographic center	Piscataquis County, 18 miles (29 km) north of Dover
Latitude	43° 4′ N to 47° 28′ N
Longitude	66° 57′ W to 71° 7′ W
Highest point	Mount Katahdin, 5,268 feet (1,606 m)
Lowest point	Sea level at the Atlantic Ocean
Largest city	Portland
Number of counties	16

Population

Population; rank (2006 estimate)	1,321,574; 40th
Density (2006 estimate)	43 persons per square mile (17 per sq km)
Population distribution (2000 census)	40% urban, 60% rural
Ethnic distribution (2005 estimate)	White persons: 96.9%*
	Black persons: 0.8%*
	Asian persons: 0.8%*
	American Indian and Alaska Native persons: 0.6%*
	Native Hawaiian and Other Pacific Islander: 0.0%*
	Persons reporting two or more races: 0.9%
	Persons of Hispanic or Latino origin: 1.0%†
	White persons not Hispanic: 96.0%

** Hispanics may be of any race, so they are also included in applicable race categories.*

† Includes persons reporting only one race.

Weather

Record high temperature	105°F (41°C) at North Bridgton on July 10, 1911
Record low temperature	–48°F (–44°C) at Van Buren on January 19, 1925
Average July temperature, Caribou	66°F (19°C)
Average January temperature, Caribou	10°F (–12°C)
Average annual precipitation, Caribou	37.4 inches (95 cm)
Average July temperature, Portland	69°F (21°C)
Average January temperature, Portland	22°F (–6°C)
Average annual precipitation, Portland	45.8 inches (116.3 cm)

State flag

STATE SONG

"State of Maine Song"

Words and music by Roger Vinton Snow
This song was adopted as the official state song of Maine on March 30, 1937.

Grand State of Maine, proudly we sing
To tell your glories to the land,
To shout your praises till the echoes ring.
Should fate unkind send us to roam,
The scent of the fragrant pines,
the tang of the salty sea
Will call us home.

Chorus:
O Pine Tree State,
Your woods, fields, and hills,
Your lakes, streams, and rock-bound coast
Will ever fill our hearts with thrills.
And tho' we seek far and wide,
Our search will be in vain
To find a fairer spot on Earth
Than Maine! Maine! Maine!

NATURAL AREAS AND HISTORIC SITES

National Scenic Trail

Maine is the start of the *Appalachian National Scenic Trail*, which follows the Appalachian Mountains from Maine to Georgia, a total of 2,174 miles (3,499 km).

National Historic Park

Maine's sole national park, *Acadia National Park*, is about 47,000 acres (19,000 ha) and covers most of Mount Desert Island off the coast of Maine. A small part of the park is on Schoodic Peninsula and another part is on Isle au Haut.

International Historic Site

Maine has two international historic sites, which are the *Saint Croix Island International Historic Site*, commemorating the French attempt to settle the island in 1604, and the *Roosevelt Campobello International Park*, which is a combined effort by the United States and Canada to protect the vacation grounds of President Franklin D. Roosevelt.

National Forests

White Mountain National Forest is the largest forested, mountainous area east of the Rockies and south of Canada. A part of this forest lies in Maine.

State Parks

Maine maintains a system of more than 30 state parks that provide year-round activities for visitors, including *Aroostook State Park*, *Ferry Beach State Park*, *Reid State Park*, and *Two Lights State Park*.

SPORTS TEAMS

NCAA Teams (Division I)

University of Maine *Black Bears*

Portland Sea Dogs

CULTURAL INSTITUTIONS

Libraries

Maine has 225 libraries. Outstanding collections are housed at the *University of Maine* (Orono), the *Maine Historical Society* (Portland), and the *Maine State Library* (Augusta).

The *Maine Historical Society* (Portland) houses Native American artifacts, as does the *State Museum* (Augusta).

Museums

The *Maine State Museum* (Augusta) preserves and presents the state's rich natural and human histories through its extensive collection.

The *Old York Historical Society* (York) is located in the oldest public building in Maine. It was built in 1653 and served as a gaol (jail) until 1860. The Old York Historical Society now houses local history relics.

The *Portland Museum of Art* has a fine collection of art by18th- and 19th-century American artists.

The *Bowdoin College Museum of Art* (Brunswick) holds important works by American artists.

The *Abbe Museum of Stone Age Antiquities* (Bar Harbor) maintains an extensive Native American collection.

The *Seashore Trolley Museum* (Kennebunkport) is the largest U.S. museum that exhibits only electric railroad equipment.

The *Tate House* (Portland) is the oldest house in Portland. This three-story wooden structure was built in 1755. It includes living quarters once used by slaves.

The *Wadsworth-Longfellow House* (Portland) is one of Maine's most popular historic sites. It was the boyhood home of the poet Henry Wadsworth Longfellow.

Performing Arts

Maine has one major symphony orchestra.

Universities and Colleges

In 2006, Maine had 15 public and 14 private institutions of higher learning.

ANNUAL EVENTS

January–June

Winter activities in Bethel, Carrabassett Valley, Greenville, Jackman, Kingfield, Rangeley, and other places (January–February)

International skiing events at Sugarloaf/Carrabassett (January–April)

Maine Maple Sunday is celebrated statewide (March)

World Mogul Invitational in Newry (March)

Moosemainea in Greenville (May–June)

Acadian Festival in Madawaska (June)

July–December

Belfast Bay Festival in Belfast (July)

Clam Festival in Yarmouth (July)

Crown of Maine Balloon Festival in Caribou (July)

Great Kennebec Whatever Festival in Augusta (July)

Potato Blossom Festival at Fort Fairfield (July)

Windjammer Days at Boothbay Harbor (July)

World's Fastest Lobster Boat Races in Jonesport (July)

Blueberry Festival in Union (August)

Lobster Festival in Rockland (August)

Maine Festival of the Arts in Portland (August)

Northern Maine Fair in Presque Isle (August)

Retired Skippers Race in Castine (August)

Fairs in Bangor, Cumberland Center, Farmington, Fryeburg, Presque Isle, Skowhegan, Topsham, Union, and Windsor (various times during the summer and in early autumn)

Chester Greenwood Day in Farmington (December)

CHESTER GREENWOOD: THE EARMUFF KING

Chester Greenwood (1858–1937) of Farmington loved ice-skating. The only problem was, his ears sure got cold. So he made two loops of wire and asked his grandmother to sew fur on them. At age 15, he had invented earmuffs! Later, he added a steel band to connect the two muffs. He called his invention Greenwood's Champion Ear Protectors, and he opened an earmuff factory. He also invented the mechanical mousetrap and the whistling teakettle!

Want to know more? See www.maine.gov/sos/kids/allabout/people/c_greenwood.htm

BIOGRAPHICAL DICTIONARY

Leon Leonwood (L. L.) Bean (1873–1967) founded the L.L. Bean company in Freeport in 1912. This mail-order and retail company sells clothing and gear for outdoor enthusiasts. Bean was born in Greenwood.

Bessabez (?–1615) was a powerful Wabanki chief who ruled over a nation of 22 villages in Maine.

James G. Blaine (1830–1893) was a prominent political figure in the 1800s. He was Speaker of the House of Representatives from 1869 to 1875 and U.S. secretary of state under presidents James A. Garfield and Benjamin Harrison. In 1884, he ran for president, losing to Grover Cleveland. Born in Pennsylvania, he later settled in Augusta.

Milton Bradley See page 100.

George Herbert Walker Bush (1924–) was the 41st president of the United States, serving from 1989 to 1993. He often spends leisure time in Kennebunkport.

Rachel Carson See page 23.

Dorothea Dix

Walter Van Tilburg Clark (1909–1971) was a novelist, poet, and short-story writer. He is best known for his novel *The Oxbow Incident*. He was born in East Orland.

William Cohen (1940–) served as the U.S. secretary of defense (1997–2001) under President Bill Clinton. Before that, he was a U.S. representative (1973–1977) and a U.S. senator (1979–1997). He was born in Bangor.

Ricky Craven (1966–) is a race-car driver. He was named Rookie of the Year by the National Association for Stock Car Auto Racing (NASCAR) in 1992 and 1995 and has placed in the top 10 of more than 40 professional races. His win in the 2003 Nextel Cup race was the closest finish in NASCAR history. Craven was born in Newburgh.

Patrick Dempsey

Barry Dana See page 73.

Patrick Dempsey (1966–) is a TV and movie actor best known for his role as Dr. Derek Shepherd in the TV drama *Grey's Anatomy*. Among his movie credits are *Sweet Home Alabama*, *Freedom Writers*, and *Enchanted*. Born in Lewiston, he grew up in Turner and also lived in Buckfield.

Dorothea Dix (1802–1878) was a reformer who worked to gain proper care and treatment for the mentally ill. She was born in Hampden.

John Ford (1894–1973) was a film director. He won six Academy Awards for films such as *The Grapes of Wrath*. Ford was born in Cape Elizabeth and raised in Portland.

Linda Greenlaw (1960–) is the fishing boat captain who was described in the book and movie *The Perfect Storm*. She has written books including *The Hungry Ocean* and *The Lobster Chronicles* about her life as a fisher.

Chester Greenwood See page 132.

Hannibal Hamlin (1809–1891) was the first Mainer to serve as U.S. vice president (1861–1865). A staunch opponent of slavery, he was vice president under President Abraham Lincoln. He also served in the U.S. House of Representatives and the U.S. Senate. He was born in Paris Hill.

James "Chico" Hernandez (1954–) was born in Chicago but graduated from the University of Maine at Presque Isle. While there, he was an outstanding wrestler and went on to serve as the team's head coach. Once featured on a Wheaties box, Hernandez is now a social worker for the Maine State Prison.

Oliver Otis Howard See page 54.

Chico Hernandez

Sarah Orne Jewett

Sarah Orne Jewett (1849–1909) was a novelist and short-story writer. Her stories are set in the seaside region around South Berwick, where she was born and spent much of her life.

David E. Kelley (1956–) is a TV producer and scriptwriter. His award-winning shows include *L.A. Law*, *Picket Fences*, *Chicago Hope*, *The Practice*, *Ally McBeal*, *Boston Public*, and *Boston Legal*. He was born in Waterville.

Stephen King (1947–) is the author of dozens of spine-chilling horror stories. Many of them have been made into movies. He was born in Portland.

William King See page 50.

Linda Lavin (1937–) is an actress who played the title role in the TV comedy *Alice* (1976–1985). She was born in Portland.

Henry Wadsworth Longfellow See page 74.

Andrea Martin (1947–) is an actress and comedienne. She won two Emmy Awards as a scriptwriter for the comedy show *SCTV*, in which she also acted. Her movie credits include *Wag the Dog* and *My Big Fat Greek Wedding*. She was born in Portland.

Robert McCloskey (1914–2003) was an award-winning author and illustrator of children's books, many set on the Maine coast. His works include *Make Way for Ducklings*, *Blueberries for Sal*, and *Time of Wonder*. Born in Ohio, he later spent his summers on Scott Island.

Carl "Stump" Merrill (1944–) is a baseball team manager. Born in Brunswick, he was a catcher on the University of Maine baseball team. He went on to manage several minor-league teams and the major league's New York Yankees (1990–1991).

Edna St. Vincent Millay (1892–1950) was a poet who was the first woman to receive the Pulitzer Prize for poetry. It was awarded to her in 1923 for *The Harp-Weaver, and Other Poems*. She was born in Rockland.

Edmund Muskie See page 85.

Judd Nelson (1959–) is an actor who appeared in such movies as *St. Elmo's Fire* and *The Breakfast Club*. He was born in Portland.

Judd Nelson

Edna St. Vincent Millay

Walter Piston (1894–1976) was a music composer and author of music theory texts. Two of his symphonies won Pulitzer Prizes. He was born in Rockland.

George Putnam (1814–1872) founded the book publishing company that became G. P. Putnam's Sons. He published books by authors such as Washington Irving and Edgar Allen Poe. He was born in Brunswick.

Edwin Arlington Robinson (1869–1935) was one of the leading poets of the 1920s and 1930s. He authored almost 30 books of poetry and won three Pulitzer Prizes. He was born in the village of Head Tide and raised in Gardiner.

Nelson Rockefeller (1908–1979) served as vice president (1974–1977) under President Jimmy Carter. Before that, he held many top political positions, including governor of New York (1959–1973). He was born in Bar Harbor.

Victoria Rowell (1960–) is an actress who has appeared in both TV and film roles. She was born in Portland.

Joan Benoit Samuelson (1958–) is a track-and-field star. She won the gold medal at the first ever women's Olympic marathon, which was held in 1984. She was born in Freeport.

Hazel Sinclair See page 58.

Margaret Chase Smith See page 84.

Samantha Smith See page 61.

Louis Sockalexis See page 78.

Olympia Snowe (1947–) is the senior senator from Maine. Married to former governor John McKernan, she at one point was both a member of Congress and first lady of the state. Snowe was born in Augusta.

Percy Spencer See page 102.

Francis (1847–1918) and **Freelan (1847–1940) Stanley** were twin brothers who founded the Stanley Motor Carriage Company in 1902. They invented a steam-powered automobile called the Stanley Steamer. They were born in Kingfield.

Harriet Beecher Stowe (1811–1896) was an author and antislavery activist. She wrote a novel about slavery, *Uncle Tom's Cabin*, which became the best-selling novel of the 19th century. She was born in Connecticut and lived for a time in Brunswick, Maine.

Louis Sockalexis

Liv Tyler

Henry David Thoreau See page 20.

Liv Tyler (1977–) is an actress. Her movie credits include *Armageddon* and *The Lord of the Rings*. She was born in New York City and spent her childhood in Portland.

Lea Wait (1946–) is an author of books for children, young adults, and adults. Many of her young people's books are historical novels set in Maine in the 1800s. Among her award-winning books are *Wintering Well*, *Seaward Born*, and *Stopping to Home*.

Elwyn Brooks (E. B.) White (1899–1985) was a writer who lived in Maine. His children's books include *Stuart Little* and *Charlotte's Web*.

Andrew Wyeth (1917–) is an artist who often paints Maine's landscapes and people. He produced his most famous work, *Christina's World*, while living in his summer home in Cushing. The Farnsworth Gallery in Rockland displays many of Wyeth's paintings.

RESOURCES

BOOKS

Nonfiction

Goodridge, Harry, and Lew Dietz. *A Seal Called Andre: The Two Worlds of a Maine Harbor Seal*. Camden, Me.: Down East Books, 1975.

Graham, Amy. *Maine*. Berkeley Heights, N.J.: Enslow Publishers, 2002.

Hicks, Terry Allen. *Maine: It's My State!* New York: Benchmark Books, 2006.

Kress, Stephen W. *Project Puffin*. Gardiner, Me.: Tilbury House, 1997.

Marsh, Carole. *Maine Indians*. Decatur, Ga.: Gallopade International, 2004.

Ross, D. J. *Uniquely Maine*. Chicago: Heinemann Library, 2004.

Thoreau, Henry David. *The Maine Woods*. New York: Penguin, 1988.

Fiction

Dethier, Vincent Gaston, and Marie Litterer (illustrator). *Newberry: The Life and Times of a Maine Clam*. Camden, Me.: Down East Books, 1981.

Howland, Ethan. *The Lobster War*. Chicago: Front Street, 2001.

Jones, Kimberly J. *Sand Dollar Summer*. New York: Margaret L. McElderry, 2006.

Stephens, Charles Asbury. *Grandfather's Broadaxe, and Other Stories of a Maine Farm Family*. New York: W. R. Scott, 1967.

Wait, Lea. *Stopping to Home*. New York: Margaret L. McElderry, 2001.

DVDs

Discoveries America: Maine. Bennett-Watt Media, 2006.
Experience Portland, Maine. 480 Digital, 2003.
The Maine Coast: A Video Tour. SITE Productions, 1995.

WEB SITES AND ORGANIZATIONS

Finding Katahdin Online: Primary Sources
www.mainememory.net/schools_FK_DocPacks.shtml
For links to maps, letters, journals, and other primary documents from Maine's history

Maine Historical Society and Museum
489 Congress Street
Portland, ME 04101
207/774-1822
www.mainehistory.org
For information about Maine's history

Maine History Told by Mainers
www.maine.gov/portal/facts_history/mainers/index.shtml
For firsthand accounts of historical events, as well as everyday Maine life today

Maine Office of Tourism
#59 State House Station
Augusta, ME 04333-0059
888/624-6345
www.visitmaine.com
For information about vacationing in Maine

Official Web Site of the State of Maine
www.maine.gov
For information on state government, history, facts, and recreation

Secretary of State's Kids' Page
www.state.me.us/sos/kids
For information on Maine's history, government, state symbols, famous people, wildlife, interesting places, and much more

INDEX

★ ★ ★

AUTHOR'S TIPS AND SOURCE NOTES

★ ★ ★

I love to travel, and visiting Maine was great fun. A special highlight of my Maine experience was visiting a boat builder's workshop. I watched him make handcrafted sailboats as he explained his centuries-old techniques. I was truly impressed by his devotion to his craft. Keeping tradition alive was much more important to him than making a lot of money.

I found some great books about Maine. Among them are *Coastal Maine: A Maritime History* by Roger F. Duncan and *The Interrupted Forest: A History of Maine's Wildlands* by Neil Rolde. *The Maine Reader: The Down East Experience, 1614 to the Present*, edited by Charles Slain and Samuela Slain, is an interesting collection of letters, essays, and poems about the state.

For further research, I especially enjoyed reading letters and journals of early settlers and seafarers in Maine. They're on the Maine Memory Network Web site (www.mainememory.net/schools_FK_DocPacks.shtml). More great first-person accounts are on the state government's Maine History Told by Mainers site (www.maine.gov/portal/facts_history/mainers/index.shtml). The secretary of state's Kids' Page (www.state.me.us/sos/kids/) is another great source of information—for grown-ups as well as kids.